Theology in Postliberal Perspective

Theology in Postliberal Perspective

DANIEL LIECHTY

SCM PRESS
London

TRINITY PRESS INTERNATIONAL
Philadelphia

First published 1990

SCM Press Ltd
26–30 Tottenham Road
London N1 4BZ

Trinity Press International
3725 Chestnut Street
Philadelphia PA 19104

© Daniel Liechty 1990

British Library Cataloguing in Publication Data
Liechty, Daniel
Theology in postliberal perspective.
1. Christian theology
I. Title
230
ISBN 0–334–02481–1

Library of Congress Cataloging-in-Publication Data
Liechty, Daniel, *1954–*
Theology in postliberal perspective / Daniel Liechty.
p.   cm.
Includes bibliographical references and index.
ISBN 0–334–02481–1: $9.95
1. Theology—20th century. 2. Deconstruction.
3. Postmodernism—Religious aspects—Christianity.
4. Authority (Religion)
I. Title.
BT83.8.L54   1990
230′.046—dc20   90–38708

Typeset at J&L Composition Ltd, Filey
Printed in Great Britain

*To the members and attenders of the
Vienna, Austria, meeting of the Religious Society
of Friends, and the Germantown Mennonite Church
of Philadelphia, Pennsylvania,
this book is dedicated in great appreciation.*

CONTENTS

For discussion of these ideas in their formative stages, I wish to thank Anatol Rapoport, Gwen Rapoport, Alexander Rapoport, Wolfgang Lassmann, Walter Sawatsky, Michael Garde, Anton Jacobs, Melvin Lehman, Clark Bell and especially my partner, Angel Chiango.

INTRODUCTION:

Approaching the Subject

Since the advent of deconstructionist thought, many fields in the humanities, from literary criticism to law, have been in the process of revolution. With its radically humanist perspective, deconstructionism casts a long shadow of doubt on the validity of the use of transcendental categories of truth and pushes to the front the political implications involved in the use of such categories.[1] The core of the revolution created by deconstruction thought is a crisis of authority. If no transcendental categories of truth, beauty and justice can be recognized to exist, then from what platform may one continue to assert the reality of these concepts? With lifetimes of careful research and writing, careers and senses of personal worth and importance at stake, it is no surprise that supporters of deconstructionist approaches have found intense opposition in the various fields of the humanities. The dissolution of a transcendent source of authority is often decried as a collapse into nihilism. This charge certainly has validity.

It is interesting to note that while deconstructionist thought has created quite a stir in every field in the humanities, news of which has even spilled over into the popular media, in the field of theology it has more or less been taken in stride. The greatest complaints and protests have come from reviewers of books upset with the obscure and jumbled prose of certain deconstructionist theologians.

For the fact of the matter is, in theological thought the process of deconstruction has been going on under different names since at least the sixteenth century. If we can characterize deconstructionism as an attempt to undermine established authority within a discipline, then it has been going on in earnest among theologians ever since Martin Luther. Of course, most theologians, Martin Luther included, only intend to undermine the authority on which their theological opponents base arguments, replacing it with some other "sure foundation" in turn. The new "mighty fortress" of authority was often backed up by the executive power of the state.

Yet the fact that these new seats of authority in religious thought had to be backed up by the executive arm of the state only demonstrates the real poverty of authority. There has never been a lack of dissidents and nonconformists to challenge new platforms of authority and anarchistically (in good deconstructionist manner) to assert that these emperors too are naked. It should not be surprising that, although for generations the theologians of America looked to Europe for leadership, deconstructionism as a specific theological approach is almost uniquely an American phenomenon. It is exactly the type of religious thinking we should expect from theologians who have been nurtured in the environment of religious pluralism and relativism. Whereas for European theologians the undermining of authority in theology has been a more or less academic problem, American religious thinkers have had to deal with it in the context of maintaining a sense of forward movement within religious institutions in an environment of a religious "free market."

I was raised and educated in a religious tradition which "officially" held that the Bible was the bottom line and unshakable authority for the church, strongly influenced by the European Neoorthodox school thought. This plays well on the congregational level. However, for a student of theology, biblical criticism and an increased understanding of hermeneutics brings one back to an axiom aimed at theology in the nineteenth century – that the proper study for human beings is the human being. This is certainly in one sense a return to the approach of classic liberal theology. Karl Barth and others were turned away from that liberal theology because of the First World War. Their criticisms of that theology are valid and are part of the heritage passed on to younger theologians. But we who are doing theological thinking in the present must also work within conditions of history which make the theology of Barth and others less convincing. While the approach in this book has definite affinities with the older "liberal" theology, it has been formulated on this side of the Barthian criticism of the classic liberal optimism about human beings and their future. To the extent that liberalism is associated with modernism, my approach is definitely "postmodern." But the meaning of postmodernism is extremely liquid at the moment and it has become something of a fad term. Hence I prefer the term "postliberal" as a description of my approach to thinking religiously.

Probably the central commitment I gained from the religious tradition in which I was raised was that of a thoroughgoing pacifism. My own struggle with the question of theological authority came as I attempted to work out a consistently pacifist theology, a theology in which pacifism in the broadest sense, of living peaceably with fellow human beings, other species, with the environment and so on, was integral to the theological frame of reference itself, and not simply one among other options reserved for the section on ethics. I hope that this outline of theology will be convincing to the reader.

I have become convinced that pacifism is ultimately anarchistic in relation to questions of authority. Authority, as the deconstructionists have reminded us, is finally a question of power. And pacifism is by nature skeptical of power. In an earlier attempt to present an anarchistic theology[2] I was still working from the perspective of the so-called biblical theology school. Therefore, while I think I was successful in formulating a theology of anarchism, I was ultimately unsatisfied with the results because I was still appealing to a specific source of external and transcendental authority for what I was writing. If that earlier attempt can be characterized as a theology of anarchism, perhaps this present attempt can be characterized as an anarchism of theology.

The question of authority in theological writing is with me at every point in this presentation. Authority, authorship, the author. I have finally come to the conclusion that authority must reside with the author. That is, the work of a theologian is similar to that of a poet or novelist. Each attempts to use words in such a way as to create a language-picture which will lead the reader to view, at least tentatively, the world in a different way. The author must hope that the reader will find in this new perspective something of value to his or her daily life. The success of a piece of theological writing depends on whether, in fact, that text does lead readers into new ways of perceiving the world of experience.

A further aspect of the context for all theological writing in our time is the very real situation of pluralism in which we find ourselves. This situation of extreme pluralism, in which ideas compete for acceptance and validation in a "free market," can be very threatening to those whose mental world is premodern in character. Deconstructionist writers have scored their main debating points by demanding that we take this situation of pluralism seriously.

Theological thought and theological writing can never assume a platform other than dialogue on all matters with which it concerns itself. However, a truly dialogical stance is not one which takes no position with respect to our religious traditions. My religious tradition is Christian. I can best bring something of value to the conversation by speaking from the perspective of the Christian tradition. But the paths of truth which I think I see from that perspective must be held out to others tentatively.

Clearly the Barthian position that "biblical faith" is somehow qualitatively different from and superior to all other "religions" simply will not do. Far less can we be satisifed with the dogma preached in the circles of fundamentalism, religious or secular.

My opinion is that a theology must be judged not only by the clarity with which it speaks of the teachings within its own tradition, but also by the respect and attitude of dialogue with which one can approach the teachings of other traditions from that theological frame of reference. The best theology will not only have room for dialogue with other traditions. It will "reach out" for such dialogue. That has been a guiding force in what is presented here. Again, I can only hope that the reader will find my approach successful in this regard.

A final word needs to be said about the style of writing chosen for this book. The "accepted" approach to theological writing is that of comparative analysis. Most theological articles and books spend an enormous amount of time explicating the writings of opponents and mustering against these the writings of those with whom the theologian agrees. I expect also to expand this book into just such a work. However, voices have been raised in protest against this kind of writing, which has the effect of excluding from the discussion all but the most academically trained people.[3] I have taken this criticism to heart and here have refused as much as possible the temptation to set up and then knock down opponents. In keeping with my view of authority and authorship, I have tried here simply to say what I have to say as clearly as possible and as briefly as possible. Likewise, footnotes have been kept to an absolute minimum. While this approach may irritate some, I hope that it will be congenial to many more.

1

A Starting Point for Religious Reflection

As consciousness of self develops, we find ourselves on this earth, living out our three-score-and-ten. It is a joy to be alive and for that we are happy. But life is not easy. Many of us have sicknesses and diseases. Many of us have deformities. There are real and genuine barriers between how we are living and how we would like to live. There is economic inequality, and the majority must work hard for a living while the few need not worry. There is oppression of the spirit and soul as well as of the body. There is injustice and fear. And in the end, death awaits. This is our situation, and it is within this context that we strive to maintain the forward movement of life. Immediately questions arise. Is this all there is to it? Can we say nothing in addition about the human condition? On what may we base our hopes?

We can only begin with a hypothesis. Human beings are an evolved species on this earth engaged in an ongoing, puzzling and at times contradictory task of grasping and understanding the whole, of which they are only a part. The main tool available for this is language. And human language is itself an artifact, a product of human community, whose origin and immediate function is itself still only dimly understood.

Human beings as a species are a result of a long and mixed evolutionary history which we share with all past and present species. We are physical beings and share completely in nature's demand that a living species maintain sources of nourishment, protection from the elements and an environment in which to procreate in each generation.

If a living species cannot maintain these in each generation, the species dies.

And species, even the mighty dinosaurs, have become extinct. Our earth is a generous mother. She provides us with all we need to flourish. Natural disasters do happen for various reasons and survival has most often been a hard struggle. In many ways human beings are more vulnerable than other animals. We are naked, weak, without instincts and in relation to an ability to survive independently are born premature. But in spite of this we have been a successful species. As we view the earth on which we live, it is possible and even compelling to give assent to the biblical assessment of the earth: And God saw that it was good.

In spite of our relative physical vulnerability as a species, we have proven ourselves able to adapt to a wide variety of environmental conditions. We have been able to vary survival strategies and continue to live in altered environmental conditions where our animal siblings, with their mighty strength, speed, sharp claws, teeth and warm coats have failed. For human beings have the greatest advantage of all species in the struggle for survival. We have powers of observation, reasoning and ability to learn new skills which exceed all of our animal siblings. We have learned to appropriate the natural gifts of our animal siblings. We cover ourselves with their warm coats and tough skins. We nourish ourselves on their muscles and milk. We make tools, weapons and ornaments of their sharp teeth, claws and strong bones. We have also mastered the laws governing plant life and can grow and store food for the future, making clothing of fiber and building shelter from wood and stone. We are indeed a very successful species, living and flourishing on a good earth.

We know that our mother the earth has not been kind to those species which could not adapt to changes in environmental conditions. Nor does the human species have unconditional hospitality promised on this earth. As a species we need not fear those "normal" natural disasters – flood, drought, earthquakes – which are an ongoing part of the earth's working. These bring terrible tragedy to specific communities but do not affect species survival. There is evidence, however, that abnormal disasters, such as a collision with large heavenly bodies, have occurred and have adversely affected the survival abilities of species now extinct. Likewise, some scientists claim that certain such occurrences are inevitable – like the sun eventually burning out – which, at a distant point in the future will make our planet uninhabitable for life as we know it. We face life, therefore, with the full knowledge that not only is each individual human being mortal, but that the species itself will one day come to an end. Our mother the earth can no more promise us life forever than a human mother can promise that to her child. Nevertheless, we can affirm of our life on this earth that "it is good."

Our mother the earth does provide us with all of the security and possibility to flourish that we could desire. To demand more of her is nothing but ungrateful *hubris*. And yet we discuss the survival of the human race now in a manner more serious than in any previous generation. Not because of the inhospitality of the natural environment has this become a real concern, but because of our own doing. In our quest to flourish on this earth, we have unlocked the secrets of the natural order which now, if we abuse this knowledge, will literally wipe us out in a short period of time. This is our own doing, for which we must take the full responsibility. The future of our race now rests in our own hands. We are no longer victims or passive agents. We are the first of species to become the architects of our future. Our physical evolutionary journey has brought us to this point and there can be no return to innocence.

We have been a successful species. On the other hand, we are relative newcomers here and the story of our success or failure is ours to finish. What will be the next chapter in the human story? Will we learn to contain the raging in our breast and create true community among ourselves and with the rest of our environment? Or will it finally be concluded that we are just one more of those curious species which have occurred during the evolutionary process, a life-form whose very characteristics which allowed them for a time to adapt successfully in the end doomed them to extinction? This is the context out of which all serious probing of the human condition must be pursued.[1]

Caution must always be taken when asking questions about human nature. Human existence is rooted in the history of particular nations, races, cultures and communities. What is assumed to be universal human nature in one context may be seen as nothing but outlandish behavior in another. The more we learn about human diversity, the more difficult it becomes to discern universals of human nature.

There are political grounds for caution as well. For the question of human nature occurs most often in challenging or justifying particular social, political and economic relations. Like appeals to special revelation from God, or more recently appeals to "scientific fact," the function of appeals to human nature is generally to cut off the discussion. It is an attempt to wield power, saying in effect, "beyond this we cannot go!" Set notions of human nature, therefore, act as ideological blinders to new possibilities.

Yet we cannot avoid discussion of human nature altogether. Like all questions of ultimate concern, the question of human nature is perennial. The best we can do is to remain aware of the tendency to ideologize such probing. What this means concretely is that we cannot forget that central to our original hypothesis is the fact that we are standing *within* the whole we are trying to grasp and understand. Therefore, even as we move into a discussion of human nature (which, by definition, is a universal concept) we must remain constantly aware that our conclusions are partial and tentative. None of us has a space outside or above the human condition from which, in the manner of the great structuralist philosophers, to make pronouncements concerning what is true absolutely. That kind of approach, characterized by Eric Voegelin as "gnosticism,"[2] has been rendered untenable by the awareness that all human thought must proceed from within particular social situations. It therefore reflects a particular social situation and is a plea for particular political responses within that social situation. In discussion of universalizing concepts such as human nature, there must be a willingness to define and defend the political responses a particular position elicits. Universalizing concepts must not be used to mask or obscure such political responses.

We know that human beings are social animals. We live together in various types of social groupings and gain our sense of identity and self-esteem within social contexts. The social arrangements are numerous, but it is only the rare individual who genuinely prefers no social interaction at all. And even they are products of a particular previous social environment. If true hermits do exist, they only prove the rule that all human actions and decisions are made in particular social contexts.

Human individuals are nurtured, for better or worse, in particular social environments and tend to internalize the values of that social grouping. These values, in turn, emerge out of the history of the particular group. Values, therefore, are products of communal existence and demonstrate the human need for community maintenance. Human values are one aspect of species survival strategy. They are encapsulations of the survival techniques of particular social groups.

If no values can claim a transcendent source, are all values relative and of equal worth? Does this not lead directly to nihilism and underscore the poverty of the type of historical-critical analysis in which we are engaged? Is it not impossible to commit ourselves to anything once we have agreed that all values are human creations, one no less so than another? There is certainly a sense in which this is true. Values, morals, restrictions and taboos, by the very fact that they have emerged out of communal existence, have represented at one point or another in the history of that community a successful survival strategy. If this were not the case, either the values would not have been adopted or the community would have perished. Therefore, while we must reject the notion that any particular value or set of values has come to human communities from a transcendent source, it is equally clear that in particular social situations some values or sets of values are useful and positive and other values or sets of values are dysfunctional and negative. The advocacy of particular values or sets of values reflect the desire to elicit certain political responses within particular social situations. Therefore, in the discussion of such values we must be willing to define and defend the political responses desired, and not use values or sets of values to mask or obscure such responses.

But the historical situation changes and values may become stagnate and counterproductive. Successful survival strategies from one period of a group's history, embodied in a particular set of values, morals, restrictions and taboos, may bring disaster when applied to new historical circumstances. If that group cannot adopt new sets of values, the people may perish.

Because we live as a species in radically new circumstances, circumstances in which our survival as a species is at stake if we continue to hold fast to the values of our culture which have brought us to this precipice, so we must be willing to critically examine even our most cherished assumptions. This includes especially those assumptions which are expressed in sacrosanct terms such as human nature and God. This is the context out of which all serious religious probing must be pursued. The task of religious thinking is therefore one in which questioning and testing is essential.[3] Particular models of God elicit certain political responses within particular social situations. We must be willing to define and defend those political responses, and not allow traditional ideas of God to mask or obscure them.

Human existence is grounded in the physical world. Survival in the physical world, for which we form community, is the bottom line of our being. But we are much more than physical beings. Human beings have powers of mind, of reasoning and ability to learn, which extend far beyond what is necessary for mere survival. This "mental overload" is the root of our creativity and is expressed in our insistence that human beings have a soul and spirit as well as a physical body.

The human soul and human spirit are not exact terms. They are even less concrete than the related word, mind. For mind connotes mental activity and that can be located in a specific organ of the body, the brain. To speak of the human soul and human spirit, on the other hand, is to speak of those aspects of the human being which can only be thought of as in distinction to the physical body. It is to speak of that aspect of human thought and experience which seems to transcend and fly far above the physical world.

We might speak of the soul and spirit, working together through the mind, as the seat of human creativity and aesthetic sensitivity. Working within the physical world, we seek to arrange what is found there so that it bears the mark of our personality. We arrange words into poems. We arrange sounds into music. We shape wood and stone into works of art and fine craftsmanship. We arrange the natural order into gardens and parks. This recognition of the creative and creating ability of human beings to shape the natural order into an expression of the human personality is surely why, in every age, the work of the artist and craftsperson has been held in high esteem. One can find no "instrumental" reason why a particular painting, for example, should be valued higher than a house. The representation itself becomes the artist's or craftsperson's only real act of (transcendent, i.e. from "outside" human history) religious conviction. And let us be honest, what these most sensitive (prophetic!) people, since at least Picasso, have been telling us, is that the optimism of the West, the belief in the progress of humanity, is without foundation.

Likewise, it is through the soul and spirit that we can appreciate the works of creativity we see in others. A purely intellectual analysis of, for example, a piece of music, is possible. But for most of us, this will never quite express what we hear in that music. While our attempts to speak of such things are necessarily fluid and imprecise, perhaps that "something more" which we recognize and appreciate when we encounter works of human creativity points towards what we mean by the human soul and the human spirit. This is perhaps also why, when we look at a beautiful sunset, the power of a gleaming waterfall, or examine the intricate structure of a living thing, it is most easy for us to encounter that beauty in terms of appreciation for a creative world spirit.

Closely related to the work of the soul and spirit in creating and appreciating beauty, that which bears the mark of our personality, is our ability to love. Giving and receiving true love is, in fact, the zenith of human creativity, that toward which we point when we speak of the human soul and the human spirit. Love breaks through the protective barriers which we erect around ourselves in fear and mistrust. It is through love that we most clearly know ourselves as a unity of body, soul and spirit. It is through love that we are able to direct most positively our creative energies. It is through love that our creative works are lifted up and invested with meaning and significance far beyond that which an intellectual analysis of those works could convey.

This is strikingly expressed in one of the most beautiful biblical passages, chapter 13 of the apostle Paul's letter to the Corinthian community. Speaking of our creative and spiritual gifts, the passage insists that without love, they come to nothing. Here love is described as always patient and kind. Love is never jealous, boastful or conceited. Love is always ready to trust and hope. Our greatest gifts as human beings, that toward which we ultimately point when we speak of the human soul and human spirit, are faith, hope and love. And of these, love is the greatest, the best, the most perfect.

Those aspects of the human experience which cannot be

reduced totally to the physical, although of course they are rooted
in the physical, are what we point to when we speak of the human
soul and the human spirit. Creativity, transcendence and love best
summarize the works of the soul and spirit. These are what we
cherish most about being human. These are what give us the sense
of being "special" in the order of nature. Our animal siblings do
not appear to possess the ability of creativity, transcendence and
love to any degree approaching that of the human being. And for
this reason we rightly distinguish and set ourselves apart from
them.

But we also know that there is something terribly wrong with us as
human beings. The very aspect of our being which sets us apart
from our animal siblings, which sets us "above" the natural order,
is also the source of our shame and disgrace as a species. Our
animal siblings kill out of instinct and for food. But we humans
kill for the purely sadistic joy of killing. Our animal siblings may
stand by while a fellow suffers out of helplessness and lack of
understanding. But only we humans purposely inflict suffering,
understanding full well what is happening, and watch that suffering with Mephistophelian fascination.

The real possibility of our extinction as a species, and many
other species with us, comes neither from our mother the earth nor
from our animal siblings, no matter how savage and wild. It comes
from us, ourselves, the crown of the natural order. That which sets
us apart from the rest of the natural order, the human soul and
spirit, the very source of our ability to create, transcend and love,
also sets a raging whirlwind in our breasts which leads us,
daemonically enchanted, toward species extinction. That by which
we may reach so high has also cursed us to sink so low. That which
can and should be our source of creativity, transcendence and love
has become our source of shame and debasement in the visage of
the natural order.

For the human being is a self-contradictory animal. In our minds
we are truly divine beings, transcendent and ethereal. In our
minds we can create new worlds or sit on the far side of the moon.
Yet this divine, transcendent, ethereal human soul and spirit is
entirely dependent on a weak and mortal physical body. After we
have created new worlds and sat on the far side of the moon, we
must inevitably return and attend to a physical body which hungers

and thirsts, defecates and becomes ill, and finally dies, taking our soul and spirit with it. A divine being who is that vulnerable! No wonder there is a raging whirlwind in our breasts!

We are indeed a curious race. Tied to a weak and mortal physical body, we spend most of our psychic energy in the creation of symbols of immortality which allows us, at least momentarily, to suppress from consciousness the fact of who we really are. Our symbols all point toward a higher allegiance, toward that which is solid, eternal and whole, toward that which is unlike ourselves, heroic and immortal. Our strivings are toward, as Ernest Becker saw so clearly, a denial of death.[4]

This contradiction in our very being is, I think, what the great religious traditions point to in the metaphor of the "fallen" state of the human condition. There is an intuitive awareness, especially during those times when we become strongly confronted with the shallowness of our symbols, that there is something desperately wrong with us as people. We will die. And in our fallen state the sting of death is painful indeed.

As far as we know, we are the only species which knows and understands the fact of death years before it actually happens. Some of our animal siblings never seem to understand death, even as the predator pounces or the butcher's blade is poised for the kill. Other of our animal siblings do seem to experience a kind of terror in the moments just prior to the mortal blow. We have all been haunted by that look of terror on an animal face. But we are a life-form who must live with that furious terror within us, now simmering, now boiling, from relatively early childhood until the day the death angel calls.

Taming this terror is, quite literally, *the* human task. If the terror could not be tamed, forward movement would simply be impossible. The person would be psychotically stunned and unable to act. Therefore, we may assume that in all but the most tragic cases, a more or less successful process of taming does occur. And this taming can take but one of two paths: that of acceptance or that of denial.

Along both paths, the mechanism of taming the terror is to create symbols of immortality, of solidity and strength, with which the person can identify and through which the person can vicariously participate in immortality. There, however, the similarity ends. For the one taking the path of acceptance, the symbols chosen as an aid in the taming process are exactly those which assist in internalizing and incorporating awareness of the self as being-toward-death. It may often be a goal for those who have chosen this path to arrive at the point where the symbols of immortality can be abandoned altogether.

The path of acceptance, of incorporation of death-consciousness into the soul and spirit, is paradoxically the path which leads to life, to a natural flowing of creativity, transcendent awareness and love. It is the path, in short, which allows human beings to maximize their potential on the earth. As will be seen, this is the path toward which Jesus Christ and other great religious figures pointed, and is the only way to make sense of the recurring paradox which appears in all of the world's great literature – that to have life, one must first lose it.

The path of denial leads in a fundamentally opposite direction. Along this path, acceptance of the fact of death is rejected as too threatening and replaced by symbols of power. Because death is encountered as an ultimate limitation, those choosing the path of denial opt for a "second reality" and channel their denial into systems and schemes of domination over nature and other human beings. This is what Nietzsche, a philospher who understood the terror of the human situation as did few others, extolled as the will to power and domination.[5] By dominating others in the limited spheres in which that is possible, one denies mortality by creating the illusion of "being more" (i.e., more being!) than those others. From childish one-upmanship games to the fullblown hierarchical structure of a tyrannical empire, the path of denial leads to a perversion of the works of the human soul and spirit. Creativity becomes destructive, while love is replaced by defensiveness, fear and suspicion. It is a zero-sum game in which gains in self-respect and life-enhancement for some must necessarily result in oppression and deprecation of others. "Eat or be eaten" is the underlying ethic of this path.

Far from holding the symbols of immortality as tentative, as aids for spiritual growth which may finally be abandoned, those taking the path of denial are forced to hold ever more tightly to their symbols. To let go would quite literally mean death for them. Their immortality symbols become idols in the most definite sense.

They are a human creation to which their creators then sacrifice themselves.[6]

The path of denial is ultimately the path of death. It creates illusions of superhumanness which are no more real than is any construct of the human mind. Yet those taking this path must quite literally invest their entire being in maintaining these illusions. They can only be maintained "on the backs" of others, thus destroying true freedom and community even while maintaining "order," and ultimately consume their own creators.

Those choosing the path of denial are most often bound to what might be characterized as a social sadomasochistic ritual, dominating in one sphere and being dominated in another: toadying up to the boss at work and then lording over weaker family members at home, so to speak. Along the path of denial, this constitutes the everyday world for most people.[7]

Along this path, the more encompassing the symbol of immortality, the more dangerous and daemonic it becomes. For symbols of immortality must inevitably clash. People participating in an immortality symbol must finally abandon it or sacrifice themselves. The more encompassing the immortality symbol, the more sacrificial can be the resources gathered to maintain it. And it is now the clash of great symbols of immortality, which we label without any sense of irony as "superpowers," that threaten ourselves and many other species with extinction.[8]

The path of denial is the easier path to take. It is the path which becomes "normal" during the socialization process in our society. As we learn to be "good citizens," we accept and internalize as our own immortality symbols those which our society offers to us: the nation, the party, success, material acquisition. And we accept the structural hierarchy, exploitation and oppression, of others, of our environment and ourselves, which is made necessary when these human constructs are invested with the significance of immortality. In the everyday world, these assumptions are rarely, if ever, questioned.

But there have always been a few who have been inadequately socialized, or who because of some other stimulus have questioned particular social fictions by which society imparts the momentary security of the path of denial to its members. Many of these people have been judged insane or worse. But they have had an insight which the rest of us must, at this juncture in our evolutionary development, take very seriously. Those who have stood against the hierarchy, exploitation and oppression of particular social constructions must become our teachers. Those who have taken the path of acceptance rather than denial must become our guides. Those who have found private resources for meaning which have allowed them to move forward in life without reliance on destructive immortality symbols must become our tutors.[9]

Private resources for meaning. Spiritual strength, taming the terror of the human condition in a constructive and loving manner. Here we stand directly before the problem of God.

2

The Ambiguity of Evil

If the present century teaches us anything, it is that the reality of evil cannot be denied or minimized. The naive notions we held about the ease and inevitability of human moral progress are now destroyed beyond repair. Faith in progress dies hard, especially for Americans, for whom it is all but inseparable from our national character. America was founded on the faith of the Enlightenment. Optimism about human possibilities has been part of that faith. If Calvinist ideas of Original Sin sobered the Founding Fathers enough to prevent the rise of an American version of the Jacobins, the combination of deistic free thinkers and religious autoinspirationists put the Tories in a small minority. At the first Continental Congress, even the conservatives were radical by the standards of that time. To speak of doubt about human progress is to speak of doubt about America's mission in the world and in human history. Even today Denis de Rougemont's essay "On the Devil and Politics" rings strange to American ears.[1]

The progressive perfecting of the human race through enlightened reason was a bedrock tenet of both the religious liberalism and the humanism of the nineteenth and early twentieth centuries. Evil was seen in the form of intolerance, disease, tyranny and inequality, the root cause of which was ignorance. Evil would be overcome by reason through education. The future could be faced with confidence, and conservative theology's doctrine of the depravity of human beings was not so much refuted as simply ignored. It was out of step with the times.

This kind of optimism, both religious and secular, is very attractive to Americans. It is an idea embodied in democracy and good old Yankee know-how! Even those fundamentalists who continued to preach sin and depravity narrowed their focus of human evil to such personal transgressions as drink, gambling, dancing and adultery. On a social level, it simply made no sense to insist on pessimism and at the same time participate joyfully in the spread of American democracy and capitalism, not to mention the "war to end all wars." Like preachers today who claim the end of the world is at hand, yet place their investments in long-term land deals, actions speak louder than words.

But our century has brought us two world wars, the rise of Nazism and Fascism, the murders of Stalinism and Pol Pot, the attempted genocide against the Jewish people, Hiroshima and Nagasaki, the Cold War and the arms race, the Vietnam War and ecological destruction. The list of atrocities continues. The reality of human evil and depravity has returned to us with a vengeance. Any system of thought, to be adequate to our time, cannot mini-mize this evil and depravity, or ignore it and hope it will go away.

Perhaps the first among those committed to an enlightened world-view who saw how deeply rooted in evil the human heart is was Sigmund Freud. Freud claimed that the goal of his science of psychoanalysis was that of replacing Id with Ego, replacing unconsciously motivated drives and actions with actions con-sciously motivated by reason. But the longer Freud delved into the human soul, the more pessimistic he became about human prospects. Building on Freud, various thinkers have tried to construct a phenomenology of human evil. Such a phenomenology must be at the center of current religious thought if it is to present a useful construction of the human situation.[2]

In the first chapter we saw that human beings are "split." We are godlike in our mental world, yet tied to death and decay in the physical world. Being conscious of death, each person calms that fear by bonding to something which gives permanence and eternal-ity. According to this basic insight concerning the nature of being human, we all want to endure and prosper and in some sense gain immortality. But knowing that we are mortal, we must strive to mask this fact of mortality and suppress awareness of it from consciousness. We seek immunity from mortality. According to Ernest Becker, it is this flight from mortality which is the driving force behind human evil.

The thing that makes [humankind] the most devastating animal that ever stuck his neck up into the sky is that he wants a stature and a destiny that is impossible for an animal; he wants an earth that is not an earth but a heaven, and the price for this kind of fantastic ambition is to make the earth an even more eager graveyard than it naturally is.[3]

Becker points to a central concept, borrowed from the literature of anthropology, which helps us to see the dynamic behind human evil. This is the concept of fetishism. The term has many meanings, but in this context it means a process by which one thing is used to symbolize another, but then eventually is treated as the thing itself. For example, wealth means goods and services. The pursuit of wealth would then mean the pursuit and accumulation of goods and services. Money might originally be seen as a symbol for goods and services or the power to command goods and services. The pursuit of.wealth would therefore logically take the course of the pursuit of money. However, the pursuit of money might indeed become an end in itself, something invested with psychological power which has little to do with goods and services. It becomes something pursued for itself. It becomes a fetish. Fetishism therefore has to do with a "narrowing down" which has become irrational. The pursuit of wealth in the form of goods and services can be seen as rational, as a part of survival, although it would surely also have a rational satiation point. (Is an electric wax paper dispenser really something for which to strive?) But the pursuit of money for its own sake, as a fetish, has no satiation point. You can always add more zeros to the ledger! There is a self-sacrifical element inherent in fetishism, for as with idolatry, that which we ourselves construct becomes the consuming focus of our life and we therefore miss the true richness of life's experience. Life becomes too narrow and constricted.

Some degree of narrowing down is necessary to human life. There is too much possible experience in any given moment not to narrow down. Even alone in one room, it would be impossible to describe fully all that it is possible to experience in that room. We inevitably must narrow down to the 'really important' things, and only these become conscious to us. Most of what is actually going on passes us by without notice. Our minds are simply not capable of taking in all that reality has to offer. A mind unable to narrow down, to fetishize to this degree, would simply be stunned by the multiplicity of everyday life.

This is even more true when we bring into view other human beings. It becomes impossible to take in all that is there to experience in the personality, the character, the individuality of each person. Just to look closely into the eyes of one other person can be momentarily immobilizing. Our minds are simply not capable of taking in all that other people have to offer. A mind unable to narrow down, to fetishize to this degree, would simply be stunned by the multiplicity of experience of other people.

But how narrowly must we narrow down? To experience life too narrowly is crippling. To experience a landscape only in terms of a prospective development site is crippling. To experience another human being only in terms of being a "client," or as a consumer, or in terms of his or her sexual organs, is crippling. It is to miss even that fullness of life which we with our limited capacity are able to experience.

It is very difficult to arrive at an agreed-upon definition of evil. But from the ways in which evil has been symbolized in human history, it is very easy to see that it primarily means death and decay, in a word, mortality. In its many forms and by its many names, evil personified, what in the Judeo-Christian tradition is called Satan, is represented by symbols of animality, death and decay.[4] Satan is pictured with animal characteristics, such as horns, hoofs and tail. Satan's abode is Gehenna, the place of the dead. The smell is that of putrification and feces. Satan's surroundings are filled with skulls and bones, vipers, dirt and filth. Satan is totally immersed in the physical world of sexual lust.

Evil has come to have, at least in our civilization, a very clear moral sense to it as well. Satan is above all wicked, the arch-enemy and opponent of good, of God. But this has not always been the case, for God also has not always had such a clearly defined moral character. Even in the biblical literature, there remain hints of a time when Satan was seen as Azazel, the god of the wilderness, a different god from Israel's god, but not necessarily evil (cf. Leviticus 16). God and Satan, good and evil, were seen as opposing but complementary aspects of reality, perhaps like the symbols of Yin and Yang in Oriental philosophy.

With the development of civilization, God, the good, began to have a more clearly defined moral character, and likewise evil, that which was contrary to the good, to civilization, also began to have a very defined moral character. Evil was seen as opposition to the will of God, as acting contrary to the law of God, as contrary to the good of society. Evil was seen as wickedness, as disorder and chaos.

We see, then, that the symbols used to describe incarnated evil, Satan, confirm the meaning of evil as death and decay, as mortality itself.

We oppose evil, and rightly so. Our aversion to evil is rooted in the attempt to escape mortality. But wait a minute! Didn't I just quote Ernest Becker to the effect than the flight from mortality is the root of human evil? We are on to something important.

We rightly oppose evil. There are very few among us who consciously embrace evil. Those who do are rightly considered to be clinically pathological. The tradition of humanism was to that extent correct when it assumed the "goodness" of human beings, when it assumed that under normal circumstances people would choose the good and oppose evil.

Reality, however, is too much for us to take in. We must narrow it down. Likewise, mortality is too much for us to oppose. And so we unconsciously narrow evil down. Mortality cannot be opposed. But lawbreakers can! There is nothing we can do to halt death. But this enemy (you name which one . . .) we can annihilate!

The basic theory here is simple. In our opposition to evil, we must of necessity narrow and focus on specific evils. Specific evils we can do something about, whereas mortality we can do little about. Our motives are good, and it is certainly better that specific evils be opposed than that no evils be opposed. However, our tendency is to become too narrow in our focus, as if "all will be well" if we can just conquer this evil before us. This becomes especially dangerous when we consider another fetishist urge, that of scapegoating, of identifying our narrowly focused evil of evils with particular persons, groups, races, ideologies.[5] Once that happens, we have lost our ability to place limits on our violence in eradicating evil. We need only then identify the eradication of evil with "God's cause" for massacre to become a sacramental act![6] The stage is thus set for the treacheries and demonic acts of our century.

Let me emphasize concisely what this theory of human evil

contends. In seeking to fight against evil, human beings bring ever more evil into the world, because all but inevitably the evil that we fight against has been too narrowly defined and too narrowly focused on other human beings and other human ideologies. As Ernest Becker put it:

> ... But if we add together the logic of the heroic [struggle against evil] with the necessary fetishization of evil, we get a formula that is no longer pathetic but terrifying. It explains almost by itself why [the human being], of all animals, has caused the most devastation on earth – the most real evil. [The human being] alone struggles extra hard to be immune to death because he alone is conscious of it; but by being able to identify and isolate evil arbitrarily, he is capable of lashing out in all directions against imagined dangers of this world. ... [The human being] is an animal who must fetishize in order to survive and to have "normal mental health." But this shrinkage of vision that permits him to survive also at the same time prevents him from having the overall understanding he needs to plan for and control the effects of his shrinkage of experience.[7]

This is exactly the frightening thing about the ambiguity of evil. We commit evil acts out of heroic intentions, the very desire to eradicate evil. It is no wonder then that generals and executioners always see themselves as working toward the "good" on both sides of a conflict! It is no wonder that people from Germany could confidently state "Gott Mit Uns" while Americans and British were just as sure that God was on their side! It is no wonder, then, that we have had trouble accepting the doctrine of the depravity of human beings and have only had its undeniability more or less forced upon us by the events of human history. For when we examine ourselves and others, what we find is not at all a desire to hurt, maim and slay, except for those who are clinically pathological. What we find is the intention to struggle heroically against evil and for the good. It is no wonder that once we begin to examine, for example in court, the "motives" for evil acts, that we find the perpetrator to have been in some way a "victim," and find some sympathy there (or else declare him or her to be criminally insane.) Human depravity must be maintained on objective grounds and not subjective grounds. In a culture in which the subjective is elevated to the position of truth, this definitely runs against the grain of the Zeitgeist. Yet this is where our century has left us.

Human beings will identify as an "enemy" that which potentially threatens personal expansion or that of the group. A fascinating book which illustrates this dynamic is Sam Keen's *Faces of the Enemy*.[8] In this book, a study of wartime propaganda which includes pages of wartime and revolutionary propaganda posters, Keen outlines a number of ways in which the enemy is fetishized and characterized as that which is fearful, threatening and in need of extermination.

In what Keen calls the "archetypes" of the enemy, we find an impressive array of images. We find the enemy characterized as the "stranger," the outsider to our group, the "them" versus us. The enemy becomes the aggressor, the guilty one in the conflict. The enemy is the faceless one, who is therefore not human. The enemy is characterized as the enemy of God, by which he is made to seem demonic. There is the enemy as barbarian, the threat to order and culture. The enemy is seen as greedy, lusting after more territory and conquest. The enemy is likened to a criminal, the perpetrator of terrorism and outlawism. As torturer and rapist, the enemy is characterized as sadist and violator. Pictured as beasts, reptiles, insects or germs, the enemy is seen as fit only for extermination. And finally, and most significantly, in pictures of skulls, bones and gravekeepers, the enemy is likened to death itself. Although Keen focuses mainly on overt propaganda posters, one unfortunately needs to go no farther than the political cartoons of the daily newspapers to find exactly such examples of these "faces of the enemy."

The apostle Paul's words take on new significance. "For it is not against flesh and blood that we wrestle, but against principalities and powers . . ." (Eph. 6) We wrestle against the power of culture to define our enemies for us, against the monopoly of society to transmit to us for our consumption fetishized images of evil which are too narrowly construed and which therefore lead us into becoming witting or unwitting perpetrators of ever more human evil. In the modern context, "wrestling with principalities and powers" must mean the process of rigorous self-criticism whereby we come to see the definitions of our culture as relative or even as lies and strive to flush these prejudices from our attitudes and actions.

We must be bold in naming these powers and struggling against them. Certainly unjust economic systems are one of these, systems which would have us believe that we have a "right" to the resources and wealth of others because we pay for them, and that the economic hopes and ambitions of others are a threat to these rights. Militarism is one of the strongest of the powers. Militarism, which begins in a legitimate urge for protection, forces on us constructions of our situation which lead to dividing the world into armed camps. Racism, sexism and homophobia also carry the power to have us falsely define evil in our world and therefore falsely divide ourselves against each other.

The media stand in our culture as one of the powers equal in demonic force to militarism. The media more than anything else transmit to us those cultural images of what is good and evil. In the grips of the profit-making system (a system which itself fetishizes reality narrowly in obvious ways) the media decide what we will see and how we will see it on a scale more massive than at any time in human history. Hiding behind the chimera of "objectivity," our televisions pipe in a constant and daily dose of glamorized violence and killing aimed not only at adults but, what is surely criminal, at our teenagers and children. Stories and facts which contradict the "official" line on world events are systematically ignored as unworthy of the news.

Especially in America, consumerism, the urge for always "bigger and better," is a definite power. Spurred by advertising, the life-blood of the mass media, people are made to feel restless and dissatisfied with what they have and to want ever more, even in a country in which by any stretch of measurement is the most materially prosperous people the world has yet produced! As with the alcoholic drinking himself to death, this urge for more must be satiated even as the resulting destruction of the environment, which is a direct result, threatens to make large areas of our land uninhabitable. The happiness that consumerism offers turns out not to be fulfillment at all, but rather a treadmill pursuit of an ever receding aspiration point.[9]

How can we who would attempt to think religiously in our time move from this analysis to theology? At the close of the last chapter we stood seeking personal sources of meaning and spiritual strength; that is, we stood before the problem of God. Has this detour, in which we have attempted to confront the reality of human evil, derailed our venture? I think not, but it should certainly sober us to the arduousness of our task. Those gods which are too easily grasped are most often the gods who preside over our heroic but evil deeds. Therefore, before we are ready to speak of God, we need yet to make explicit the parameters which our confrontation with human evil sets for our discussion.

We know that we have the tendency to define too narrowly the focus of evil. Among other things, this leads us to see the "demonic" in the face of the enemy. We know that a narrowing down of the multiplicity of experience is necessary for forward movement. But it is a necessary tendency we must necessarily struggle against. Therefore, any gods which justify our demonization of other human beings must be treated with absolute suspicion. Those gods which aid us in expanding our vision of reality and which lead us to reconcile ourselves to those from whom we have been alienated, those who we have seen as "them," must be considered true. A true God leads one to self-criticism, a wrestling with the principalities and powers.

I stated in the introduction that one thing I have retained from my own religious background is a very strong commitment to pacifism. I now justify that stand on grounds much more complex than the justification which came from that upbringing. In the context of the present analysis, I hope that one of these justifications will now make sense. We know that we have an heroic urge to move against evil. But we also know that we have a necessary drive to define evil in narrow and manageable channels. This leads us to identify "evil" with the ideologies, actions and being of other concrete human beings. In this we are greatly influenced by the Pauline principalities and powers of cultural transmission. In short, we can never be sure in any absolute sense that that which we have identified as evil and those whom we have identified as evil are in fact evil, and not simply our fetishistic illusion of evil. In fact, all of history points us towards the conclusion that we are probably wrong, and that our move against the evil we see will simply lead to even more evil.

Yet it would be wrong simply to throw up our hands and give sanction to the evil we see. Therefore we need to move against evil, but must struggle to do so in ways that make it least likely that we will thereby add to the evil which already exists. More elucidation of how this works politically is a topic for discussion of its own. In the meantime I want to say that for me, pacifism means, above all else, a sort of political application of the Hippocratic maxim, "Above all, do no harm." In other words, at that point in our struggle against evil when we would feel justified to kill, maim or slay another human being, signal flags should stand out on our mental horizon that warn us that we have constricted our view of evil too narrowly and have scapegoated the cause of evil exiguously. It is at that point where self-criticism is needed, where we must further wrestle with principalities and powers, before we are ready to resume the struggle against evil. Failure to do so at that point must inevitably lead one into becoming yet another perpetrator of the atrocities of human history. To act as a pacifist in the move against evil at least makes it much less likely that one will do great harm.

Only a God who helps us to expand our vision, who leads us toward reconciliation with the enemy, who assists us in the task of self-criticism, the wrestling with the principalities and powers of our world, is worthy of attention in the modern context.

3

God in the Nexus of Human History

Throughout the history of the human race, probing questions of ultimate concern have focused on religion and the problem of God. The human situation places a heavy burden of fashioning meaning for our lives out of the raw data of personal and collective experience. In the context of what we have previously said about the human situation, it is quite clear why the problem of God is perennial for human beings. For however God is conceived, God represents at minimum a vision of a "perfect" being. God is a concept expressing what it would be like to have creative and transcending mental and spiritual characteristics which are not limited by the human characteristic of physical mortality. God is our highest immortality symbol.[1]

God represents a resolution to the contradiction we human beings feel within us. We are "split" beings. God is whole, perfect. At minimum, God is a construct of the transcending human mind, a creative expression of the solution to the human dilemma. God is the spirit's ultimate goal in the quest for creating meaning in the human situation. We come closest to experiencing a person's deepest emotional longings when we encounter that person's image of God.

Because the construction of a concept of God emerges directly from the quest for meaning, it follows most naturally that one of the aspects we attribute to God is that of *Creator*. Integral to the quest for meaning is a satisfying answer to the question "from where do we come?" We are historical beings. The meaning we find in human community cannot be separated from a knowledge that our present is grounded in a significant past.

On one level, we see evidence of this spiritual need in the search for "roots," and the current fad of geneological research. It is not surprising that it is exactly in those societies most atomized that the geneologist is kept most busy. For when participation in the social community itself is no longer able to inspire a deep sense of purpose, individuals will seek to find that sense of groundedness in personal family history.

On another level, the historian works to create a story which enables a particular community or nation to take hold of a sense of purposeful past. Our best historians are those who weave a pattern of coherent meaning from the past without resorting to uncritical hagiography or myth.

At yet a different level, evolutionary scientists seek to unlock the mystery of the origins of species, the earth and the universe itself. While it is sometimes difficult for the nonspecialist to follow the intricate reasoning of these scientists concerning their conclusions, there are very few who have no fascination in the museum exhibits and media programs which are the fruits of this type of research. That whole communities of our most gifted people devote their lives to this research is itself evidence of the importance we place on the question "from where?" for our construction of a sense of meaning and purpose.

But the human soul and spirit want more than this. Understanding the mechanism of evolution can only go so far in satisfying the quest of the soul and spirit for meaning and a sense of purpose. In the final analysis, we are seeking an answer qualitatively different from that which the theories of science can provide. It is in answer to this qualitatively different question that the meaning of the attribute of God as Creator is found. It is not simply in answer to yet another round of "then where did that come from?" that human beings are led to ponder the concept of God as Creator. Ascribing the attribute of Creator to our construct of God is, rather, an almost Promethean insistence of the human soul and spirit that we *will* find meaning and purpose in this universe, in our mother the earth, in human community and in our individual lives.

Scientific theories of the origins of the universe must assume that random events plus chance account for "why" there is a universe rather than no universe – why there is something rather than nothing. The same is true for such theories as to the origins of life on this planet. We cannot easily return to a cosmology in which the earth was seen as the center of the universe and the universe existed primarily for the benefit of the human race. Human pride has been leveled b the scientists' theories and findings. Random events plus chance may indeed be the "reason" we are here. But our ascribing the attribute of Creator to God expresses the strong suspicion we have that, at least in this case, the dice was loaded.

Historical purpose embraces necessarily not only a sense of rootedness in a meaningful past, but also a sense of direction for the future. Therefore, because a construction of the concept of God emerges directly from a quest for meaning, it follows naturally that another aspect we attribute to God is that of *Sustainer*.

Because we feel the split in our being between the transcending abilities of the mind, soul and spirit and the mortality of the physical body, any reflective human being will also at various times experience an intolerable and terrifying sense of the insecurity and "suspendedness" of life. The logicians' argument that just because the sun has risen every morning up till now is no proof it will rise tomorrow may strike many of us as ivory tower nonsense. But who among us has not felt the shock of loss and has been thrown back upon questions of ultimate concern by the tragic death of a loved one or some other stark reminder of the frailty of our very lives?

We rebel at the fragility of our lives, our relationships, our emotions. Yet where may we turn to make sense of things, to find meaning, in these times of deep despair?

The inquiring mind at its best seeks to understand the material causes of human suffering and despair. We seek, for example, through medical research and other such avenues to create the resources necessary to minimize the tragedies which imperil our life on this earth. That whole communities of our most gifted people devote themselves to this type of research and care is evidence of the need we have to ensure that human life be sustained.

Yet the sense of existential anxiety that sudden tragedy provokes cannot fully be comforted by the heroic efforts we make to minimize human suffering. It is comforting to know that less people will die of, for example, cancer than has been the case up till now. But the tragedy of *particular* cases of suffering is not lessened by that fact. The human soul and spirit senses the limitless worth of each person and continues to pose the question, "What about *this* person, my parent, sibling, friend, lover, suffering and dying? How can I make sense of that?" It is here that a qualitatively different answer is needed than can be supplied by our efforts to minimize human tragedy. Only submission in the knowledge that through the love of our sustaining God will "all things work together for good" can possibly comfort our grieving soul and spirit in such times of despair.

This is neither the Pollyanna blindness of this as the "best of all possible worlds," nor the bland posture of abandoning all to that random and impersonal entity called Fate. Ascribing the attribute of sustainer to our construct of God is a cry of the human soul and spirit that, in the full face of the tragedy of life, we *will* find meaning and purpose in the universe, in our mother the earth, in human community and in our individual lives.

We live at the close of what has been called the "modern" era. This is an era in which human consciousness is characterized by a strong separation or distinction between the human sphere and the sphere of nature. In premodern times it would have been very difficult for any human being to conceive of himself or herself as completely distinct from the order of nature and to view the natural order in purely instrumental terms. The modern consciousness of historicism and individualism, which made possible the development of the capitalist mode of production and was in turn furthered by that mode of production, created an environment in which wealth was fabricated at a level never before seen in human history. In no previous time did human beings understand the material abundance available to us, hidden in the sphere of nature. By harnessing the power of nature and exploiting nature's raw materials, modern societies became extremely wealthy.

This mode of producing wealth brought with it a radical change in the consciousness of human beings. It tore apart completely any connection the human being might feel with nature and imposed upon nature a standard of value created by the capitalist mode of production. In modern society, a giant redwood tree would henceforth not be seen as an awesome creation of nature to be appreciated and contemplated. It would be seen only as containing so many board-feet of building material. Chop it down, saw it up and sell it. All values in modern society tend to become instrumental values, reducible to a figure on a page. Any resistance to such valuation, any sphere of life one hopes to protect from such calculations, is only because of residual "sentimentalism."

We are presently in a transition between modern and postmodern consciousness. The capitalist mode of production which formed the foundation for the modern consciousness has contained and aggravated social stratification in the distribution of labor and wealth. Justification for this was found in the doctrine of private property. Property rights and the right to accumulate more property have been an unquestioned value in modern society. It has been taken for granted in our society that such accumulation is justified. Many of the values of modern society are positive and are rightly held in high regard. The demystification of nature, allowing scientific investigation and discovery, and the value and rights of the individual, are the most obvious of these.

On the other hand an increasing number of people are realizing that the values thrust upon us by the capitalist mode of production have a very high cost. Individual self-interest is pursued even at the risk of destroying the fabric of our ecology. Community environments are plundered by "developers" on the one hand and economic dislocation on the other. And what is left is plundered by the drug-pushers. From a strictly modern point of view, it is difficult to criticize this environmental destruction. It is an unintended result of individual pursuit of property. Yet we see that it is objectively wrong. So many people are recognizing that the values of modern society are stagnant. People have begun to see that a distinction is needed between holding individual rights in high esteem and giving simple license to egotism. People are seeking a frame of reference in which such a distinction can be made.[2]

Faced with these problems, many people long for the "good old days," a time when order and neighborliness was supposedly taken for granted. It is questionable whether the "good old days" ever actually existed. Certainly they did not in the ideal state in which they are now remembered. But our tendency to idealize the past – whether that be the 1930s, the seventeenth century or even the Middle Ages – does illustrate our awareness that the values thrust upon us by the modern era are not unambiguous. It repeats a pattern, a recurring theme in all religion, literature and tradition, that the present is "fallen" or degenerate when compared to a glorious past.[3]

We can appreciate the demystification of nature and the championing of individual human rights. But we also recognize that modernity, which views all things, including human relations, strictly in instrumental terms, has finally placed us at war with each other and at war with the natural order. This has been destructive of the human quest for meaning, in spite of greatly enhanced wealth. Therefore, as we move into a postmodern era, we also attribute to our model of God the attribute of *Unifier*. God is that cosmic voice who calls us into supra-individual community with each other and with the natural order. God is the embodiment of our motivation to seek unity beyond the egotistical individualism of modernity.

This is neither a pantheistic remystification of nature nor a regressive subsuming of the individual into the tribe. It is the profound unity of love, a reflection of the human desire for creative transcendence over and beyond modernity, a modernity which was so prophetically described by Marx and Engels in the *Communist Manifesto* as drowning all of our highest moral sensitivities in "the icy waters of egotistical calculation." It reflects our growing awareness that values which set us against each other and against the order of nature are stagnate. If these values were progressive and helpful in one period of our history, they have become destructive to our quest for meaning now. By ascribing the attribute of Unifier to God, we give an almost Promethean expression to our desire that, in spite of the instrumental values thrust on us by modern society, we *will* find hope and meaning in human community on this earth.

God is conceived differently in different traditions. But we find unity in these many conceptions, in that God is posed as an answer to the human condition, more or less satisfying, but in any case the best we can do. God reflects the deepest longings of the human soul and spirit. In God we find a more perfect reflection of the creativity, transcending personality and love which is the fruit of the human soul and spirit. In God the human soul and spirit find strength to move forward in love, even in the full face of human tragedy.

But just as creativity, transcendence and love are the natural fruit of the human soul and spirit, for those choosing the path of denial these are perverted. The person is drawn instead to symbols of immortality based on power. Then the image of God, a reflection of the soul and spirit, suffers the same perversions. For those following the path of denial, analogies used in a construction of God can only be based on extrapolations from the hierarchical structures of power. God is seen as the judges' judge, the warriors' warrior, the kings' king, the tyrants' tyrant, the apex of the pyramid of power. God is conceived as an omnipotent ruler who lords it over even the lords and princes of the earth. God becomes that terrible Being seeking to punish, satisfied only with Godself, whose love is unloving and whose justice is unforgiving. Obey this God or else!

This God can be nothing other than mutually supportive of an oppressive *status quo*. This God is the special preserve of the powerful, the rulers and kings, a God who places the divine stamp of approval on whatever actions bully nations of this world perceive to be in their own selfish interest. This is the God of nationalism, the God who is "on our side" in any and all conflicts, a God for whom reflective self-criticism would be impossible.

It is impossible in the final analysis to establish a personal and loving relationship with such a God. Fear and servitude are the only possible attitude. Ultimately, while giving us illusions of power and direction, this God is defeating of the human quest for purpose and meaning. For a God who acts capriciously, unlovingly, unforgivingly, is no different from that blindness which sees this as the "best of all possible worlds" (best, that is, for those who benefit from the present systems of oppression, who say, "how can this be wrong? your oppression is an illusion, we are really your benefactors, it is God's Will that it be so . . ."). Or it is no different from the bland posture of abandoning all things to that random and impersonal entity called fate (that is, for the rest of us, who say, "my oppression is my own fault, I must have done something to deserve it, I am less like God than the rulers, rewards will come in the next life, it is God's Will that it be so . . .").

Human values are the product of particular historical circumstances. These values, mores, restrictions, and taboos have a specific survival value in specific circumstances. As circumstances change, so must the values of a community change. If values stagnate and the community holds tenaciously to these stagnant values, the people may perish. It is likewise with our conceptions of God.

Our constructions of God are a reflection of the deepest longings of the human soul and spirit. Images of God, conceptions of God, like human values, are specific to specific historical circumstances. Because our image of God sets those parameters of human response to our circumstances, a stagnant construction of God, like a stagnant value system, may produce tragic results.

Those taking the path of acceptance are best able to perceive the need for new formulations of community values because they regard present community values as tentative. They will view present community values as opportunities and tools for constructing environments of freedom within which the creative, transcending and loving works of the human soul and spirit may prosper. Because these values are held to be a means to a different end, it is possible to notice when these values hinder rather than foster the achievement of that end.

Those following the path of denial are least able to perceive the need for new formulations of community values because they regard present community values as absolute, as ends in and of themselves. Their entire immortality project is inextricably bound to an insistence that the *status quo* must, at all costs, be maintained. Because these values are held as absolutes, it is impossible to notice if the values are tending to hinder rather than foster the creative, transcending and loving works of the soul and spirit. When present values are held as absolute, anything which suggests otherwise is a threat. When the creative, transcending and loving soul and spirit begin to contravene the utopia of the *status quo*, the only apprehension of the situation which is possible is that it is chaotic, wicked, anarchist, blasphemous. To admit any other possibility would quite literally mean death to that one who has chosen the path of denial.

It is the same with our constructions of God. Those taking the path of acceptance are best able to perceive the need for new conceptions or models of God because they hold present models to be tentative, a means to a different end. There is freedom and mutuality in relation to any particular model of God. They will view present constructs as tools for building environments of freedom within which the creative, transcending and loving works of the human soul and spirit may prosper. Because these models of

God are held to be a means to a different end, it is possible to notice when these constructs hinder rather than foster the achievement of that end.

Following the path of denial, there can be only servility and obsequiousness in relation to a particular construction of God. The image is held to be static, absolute, an end in itself, beyond the challenge of the human soul and spirit. Those on this path are least able to perceive the need for new formulations of God because they hold one particular construct as absolute, as an end in and of itself. Their entire immortality project is inextricably bound to an insistence that the *status quo* must at all costs be maintained. Because this construct is held as absolute, it is impossible to notice if it tends to hinder rather than foster the creative, transcending and loving works of the soul and spirit. When one model is held as absolute, anything which suggests otherwis is a threat. When the creative, transcending and loving soul and spirit begin to contravene the utopia of the *status quo*, the only apprehension of the situation which is possible is that it is chaotic, wicked, anarchist, blasphemous. To admit any other possibility would quite literally mean death to that one who has chosen the path of denial.

What are we saying here? Is God, after all, nothing but a human construct, a word game, an illusion? What about Godself? Does God *exist* or not? Having listened to what has been said so far, the skeptic has every reason to throw down the gauntlet, saying, "Look, if God exists, then God exists quite apart from human conceptions of God. Present your evidence for God's existence and I will make my decision pro or con based on that evidence!"

The fact is, there is no way to answer this directly. If God were an entity demonstrable by evidence, theological construction would be unnecessary. We can, however, make a few observations which at least shed some light on the nature of this type of skeptical challenge.

First, for both the one along the path of acceptance and the one along the path of denial, God reflects the deepest longing of the soul and spirit. God is a symbol of immortality. God is the human mind's projection of perfection, the human soul and spirit's insistence that, even in the full face of the tragedy of existence, meaning and purpose can and must be found. God is our assurance, in the face of despair, that our quest for meaning and purpose has a goal and is itself meaningful. This is circular reasoning, to be sure, as must be every probing of ultimate concern. That predicament is one aspect of what we accept when we accept the human situation as mortal and finite.

Secondly, the skeptic's demand for evidence is based on a particular mode of logic which has flowered in modernity. It has become part of what Antonio Gramsci referred to as the hegemony of common sense.[4] This hegemony is a ruling-class preserve. Religious skepticism, as well as credulity, can serve the purpose of maintaining the *status quo*. Just as our notions of God set parameters for human response in particular situations, so too does atheism. Therefore, in particular social situations, taking a position for or against the existence of God is an attempt to elicit certain political responses. A discussion of the existence of God cannot, therefore, take place in a vacuum. The political consequences of a position for or against must be examined in the context of particular circumstances and judged on the basis of the political response each position elicits in those circumstances. In short, since no one denies that objects of ultimate concern are real, it is always in each particular circumstance that the discussion actually takes place on the question of *which* God(s) exist(s) or not.

Thirdly, whether or not one accepts the word "God" in the context of the deepest longings of the human soul and spirit, all reflective people must continue to search for answers to perennial questions of ultimate concern. An open but hardnosed skepticism is always in order. This skepticism helps us to always hold any particular model of God as tentative. But atheism or agnosticism do not lead automatically to the path of acceptance. Rejection of God has often led only to treating as absolute some other human institution, such as the state, the party, an ideology, wealth, power. How does one hold such "absolutes" as tentative? There is no forward movement if God is debunked, only to have the void filled by an entity even more clearly "human" in origin. The free and open person would do better to give final assent to that which is the highest construct of the human soul and spirit than to that which is less than the highest.

Finally, it has to be stressed that God is not a table or a chair, or even an energy field. We cannot expect to find evidence for the

existence of God by methods resembling evidence for the existence of mundane objects. God's existence is inextricably linked to
the way people live. A particular construct or model of God is not
"true" because it accurately describes an object to which it
corresponds. The world is determined by the eye of the artist, not
vice versa! The truth of any particular construct of God can be
maintained only by the fact that it does indeed set parameters for
human response in particular situations which create an environment of freedom within which the creative, transcending and
loving works of the human soul and spirit may prosper.

That there should also exist a Being which corresponds to,
attracts, the deepest longings of the human soul and spirit is
obviously a form of wish-fulfillment. We have, as critical thinkers,
learned to be cautious in evaluating evidence presented on a
subject in which the one presenting has a strong personal interest.
Concerning the problem of God, that includes all of us! The idea
of God is surely wish-fulfillment, that is true. We can take some
comfort in the knowledge that sometimes human desires and
hopes also correspond to reality. In other words, just because we
would like it to be so doesn't necessarily make it *not* so. We could
simply ascribe "existence" as an attribute of God, as was done by
Anselm and the ontological tradition. But that won't make it so
either. Our reason can only leave us with an open question on this
point. Belief is possible, but can be explained only on the basis of
circular reasoning.

We simply cannot know Godself in any way that bypasses
historical means. Godself remains closed to us. We are inextricably bound within the nexus of our humanity for expressing and
assessing our images, constructs and models of God. Therefore,
whatever Godself is or is not, our constructs of God are human
constructs, and subject to the varieties of human historical and
social existence. We are responsible for the content we give to our
theological constructions.[5] We must be clear on this point.

If all of our ideas about God are human constructs, how can one
be better than another? Are they not all essentially the same?
Does this not prove, once and for all, that we have set ourselves
afloat on a sea of relativism with nothing to anchor to? Is not
nihilism the only realistic understanding of our situation?

As a symbol of immortality, different models of God function in different ways, setting different parameters for human response in particular situations. There are constructs of God which foster the creative, transcending and loving works of the soul and spirit. It is to this that our great teachers have pointed us when they have encouraged us to seek God within ourselves, to seek God in the creativity, transcendence and love which is the fruit of the soul and spirit. To know this God, to know thyself, to know the Law which is written on the heart, recognizing the Kingdom of God among us, is to know truly the God, by whatever name, who fosters the freedom of the human soul and spirit and gives confidence to act, even in the full face of human tragedy, according to the soul and spirit's creative, transcending and loving promptings.

There are also constructs of God which stifle the freedom of the soul and spirit, which produce only an anima of fear, self-doubt, mistrust, servility and abasement. Such images of God are the manipulative tools of the powers of oppression in this world. The true believer stands with the skeptic in an attitude of atheism toward these latter constructs of God.

We are responsible for constructing models of God which foster the works of the soul and spirit, and for debunking those models of God which pervert the works of the soul and spirit. Just as it is now in our hands to write the next chapter of the human story, just as we can no longer perceive ourselves as passive victims of the evolutionary process, so it is that God comes to an Omega Point. God, now inextricably incarnate in human history, becomes our responsibility also. We must choose the God we will serve!

The biblical God is one God who places the choice squarely in front of us. This is a God whose name is "I am who I am" (or "I will be who I will be") and *not* who the powerful, the oppressors, those who control the hegemony of common sense, say that I am. This is a God, the Creator and Sustainer, who stands with the oppressed against the utopia of the *status quo*. This is a God who was adopted by a strange people, a federal union of rebellious peasants and runaway slaves. It is this God who places the choice squarely in front of us. "Choose this day whom you will serve!"

No, all images of God are not equal. We must apply a functional political hermeneutic in accepting or rejecting a particular model of God. Whose interests are supported by a particular construct of God? Whose "truth" do we confront there? Our preference for one construct over another, accepting as God's attributes certain aspects while rejecting others, is finally a statement of personal commitment about which side one stands on in the ongoing struggle between freedom and servitude. In this context, the most discussed "preferential option for the poor" has a very direct and critical consequence for theological reflection. For it is among the victims of unjust economic structures, of sexism and racism, of homophobia, that we hear those expressions of doubt and dissent, of principled atheism, toward current constructs of God which are supportive of an oppressive *status quo*.

A final point needs to be made on the consequences of constructing models of God. God represents our idea of a perfect being. Therefore, while we must construct models of God, and in that sense stand "above" God, the construction itself reminds us that *we are not God*. Therefore, even for a community fully conscious of its own role in theological construction, it is always pure idolatry ever to assume that we and we alone speak or act in God's name, as if our will and the will of God were synonymous.

Likewise, because we are not God, we are not God equally. As human beings, we all stand in a state of equality before our theological models. The image of God functions as a powerful leveling idea. It stands as an opposing force to any human pretension which would have us believe that "some are more equal than others."

Here we have probed some of the implications of the idea of God being fully incarnate in human history. This brings us now into direct encounter with that carpenter's son of Nazareth in whom Christian faith sees this incarnation in a special instance.

4

The Example of Jesus

Critical reflection on the nature of human thought, language and reasoning forces us to recognize that all of human existence is contained within the nexus of historical particularity. This realization is both frightening and liberating. It is frightening because we human beings know just how weak, how naked, how ill-prepared we are to face the radical responsibility this places on our shoulders.

There can be no expectations of aid *ex machina* which will step in and remedy our situation if we fail to act responsibly. Our mother the earth will yield her fruits only if we respect and work within the natural order. But if in greed we violate that natural order, the earth will cease to be a friendly environment within which to prosper as a species. Forests saturated with acid rain will die. A polluted environment will remain uninhabitable, unable further to accommodate our species. Eroded top soil in our farmland will not soon be replaced. An environment spoiled by nuclear war will not soon be reclaimed for humankind. As far as we can tell, the universe will be totally indifferent to our fate if we persist in spoiling the natural environment. There can be no expectation of a cosmic force which will stay the hand of humankind should we decide to commit collective suicide. We and we alone will finish the story of our species.

But this realization is also liberating. For it removes us once and for all from the status of passive victims of forces over which we have no control. We can, if we will, create a positive and meaningful future for our race. There is nothing keeping us from this other than the perversions of truth in our own collective soul.

Furthermore, we have the very resources within us which we need to choose that positive and meaningful future. The creative, transcending and loving proddings of the human soul and spirit are ours to employ if we only still the raging whirlwind within our breast long enough to heed our inner promptings, to the voice of "the Law as written on our hearts." We recognize now no less than in the "age of belief" that the human struggle is finally a spiritual warfare. What separates us from the people of the age of belief is not their perception of the battle as spiritual and our perception of the battle as something else. What separates us from them is our recognition that the spiritual warfare is not between reified cosmic forces of good and evil which allowed a human escape from responsibility in the posture of passive victim between these forces. Rather, we know that the spiritual warfare rages solely and only within ourselves. We decide the outcome and must accept both the responsibility and the consequences of our choices.

We can no longer see God as "out there," dispassionately viewing the cosmic panorama. If such a Being exists, that Being is irrelevant to our concerns. The only God who can save us from our predicament is that God whom we construct, a God whose function in our lives is to foster an environment of trust and freedom within which the creative, transcending and loving works of the human soul and spirit are encouraged and prosper. We alone may construct this image of God. This God is, therefore, fully incarnate in human history. Only this God is able to "act in history." But this God may act only as a consequence of our actions, our choices, our willingness to seek and act upon the creative, transcending and loving proddings of the human soul and spirit. Seeking the Spirit in each generation is no longer something reserved for the "religious" among us. It has become for each of us the only species survival strategy possible.

This understanding of God fully incarnate in human history inexorably leads the Christian back to contemplation of Jesus Christ, the Nazareth carpenter's son, through whom the Christian tradition has applied the symbol of incarnation in a unique way. In the context of our understanding of God's incarnation in human history, how may that carpenter's son encounter us today?

Jesus of Nazareth was born into a worker's family of Palestine, a land suffering under the yoke of Roman military occupation. The

traditions surrounding his birth quite intentionally and deliberately picture this Jesus, this one whom many would recognize as
God's Messiah, God's Anointed, as not being born into the circles
of prestige and power in that society. There is nothing about the
circumstances of this birth which would lead us to expect "great
things" of this child. God, in anointing this child as a chosen
vessel, was once again confounding the hegemony of the *status
quo*.[1]

This confounding of an oppressive *status quo* has a long history
in that peculiar people among whom Jesus was born. It is a history
which explicitly illustrates both the possibilities of the path of
acceptance and the perversions of the path of denial.

Modern sociological research into the origins of this peculiar
people, the Hebrew nation, indicates that it emerged from a
federal union of two main groups.[2] One of these was a loosely constructed alliance of peasants and mercenary soldiers in Palestine
who were in rebellion against the feudal oppression of the city
states in the region. Like the city dwellers, these peasants
worshipped the god El. The other main group was made up of
former slaves who fled from Egypt into Palestine. These runaway
slaves, holding to traditions of Mosaic leadership, worshipped the
god Yahweh.

The union of these two groups was made possible by the fact
that each recognized in the other the common characteristic of
rebellion against an established authority of political heirarchy.[3] It
was fundamental to the historical experience of both groups that
the system of kingship meant, for them, only oppression. Their
union into one people was based on an explicit and institutional-
ized intention that, among themselves, there would be no such
authoritarian political office to lord it over the rest of the society.
The alternative they developed to the system of kingship was a
clan-based tribal federation in which united national policy was
subject to the voluntary compliance of the tribes.[4]

The tribes united under a religious cult administered by one of
the tribes, who for that reason was kept landless, to guard against
the simultaneous accumulation of wealth and religious authority in
the hands of one tribe. Because of the diverse cultural background
of the people, the bonds of cooperation were not easily developed
and had to be continually reaffirmed. Their vision of a society free
from the oppression of tyranny moved them forward. The function

of the religious cult was to be a mechanism of that affirmation of unity and cooperation.

The god of this religious cult was constructed from the religious traditions which the two groups brought with them from before the formation of the union. A new image of God was constructed from these diverse traditions, the image of the LORD GOD (Yahweh Elohim – or simply Yahweh). This God was characterized not only as Creator and Sustainer, but also with moral partisanship in favor of the weak. Most important, the kingship of this God was not mediated by a human despot. The immediate kingship of God was truly an innovation in the people's theological development and stood as a buffer against tendencies to forget the original social vision and appoint a human king. The power of this God was experienced among this people not through the structures of political heirarchy, but in the immediate experience of equality, mutual aid and cooperation among themselves.

Eventually this people did forget the social vision which had empowered and facilitated their original union as a people. After some generations of living in the clan-based tribal federation, the demand for a human king did arise among them. A human king was indeed appointed. Yet even in the texts reciting the history of this decision (which were edited in the king's court!) strong indications remain that suggest this was a fundamentally wrong decision.[5] The image of God as the God who exalts the lowly and throws down the powerful remained with the people in the preaching of their prophets and constantly undermined and relativized the pretensions of the king and his ruling class to absolute power.

The experiment with a hierarchical political structure using the kingship model proved to be a total disaster. It very soon cost the people their unity, with the nation splitting into two separate political entities. In this state of disunity they were easy prey for more powerful neighboring nations. First the Northern kingdom was conquered and sent into exile, where they became lost to history. And finally the Southern kingdom was also conquered and sent into captivity.

But among the exiles of the Southern kingdom, the people were able to construct a new image of God which in the end allowed them to survive as a people, in spite of their exile. Those attributes of God as the God of the weak, opposing the strong, were given renewed emphasis. Furthermore, this God was affirmed as a God whose love and concern, whose care for the people, was independent of their possession of the land.

There had long been inclinations in the religious traditions of the people to ascribe universality to their God, to claim their God as the only true God. These inclinations proved disastrous during the period of kingship because despite the warnings of the prophets it led to illusions of invincibility, to illusions that this God would provide the divine stamp of approval on whatever the political state perceived as being in its own best interest. These nationalist illusions were dashed by the conquering Assyrian and Babylonian armies.

But now, among a weak and defeated people in exile, the attribute of God's universality was reinterpreted in an affirmation that God is God over all the kingdoms of the earth, even as these kingdoms rise and fall. To honor this God as God was a higher allegiance and duty than to honor and serve any of the princes and kings of the earth. Thus the early anti-kingship currents on which the people were founded re-emerged in the period of exile in a new construct of the image of God. This God relativized and undermined the pretensions to power and grandeur of all the princes and kings of the earth.

This new construct of the image of God was built principally on the currents of anti-kingship present from the foundation of the people; on the ancient image of God as having special concern for the weak and powerless against the powerful, which was preached by the prophets during and after the period of kingship; and on the currents of the universality of God, tempered and reinterpreted in light of the disastrous experience of human kingship. This new construct of the image of God allowed the Hebrew people of the Southern kingdom to maintain group identity not only in the period of the Babylonian exile, but also in diaspora, when they spread all over the Mediterranean world. This pure monotheism has remained a central element in exposing and undermining the pretensions to power and glory of the powerful since that time, even into the present.[6]

Central to the expression of this new image of God was the promise that God would one day anoint a servant who would bring in God's true kingdom in such a way that the kingdoms of this earth would be superseded and a new era of God's immediate kingship would be recognized by all of humankind. This would be for all people a time of freedom from material scarcity and political oppression. Wars would cease and the creative, transcending and loving works of the soul and spirit would prosper.

It is the confession of the Christian faith that that promised one who would inaugurate this Kingdom of God is none other than the lowly carpenter's son, Jesus of Nazareth.

The enduring message of Jesus is the affirmation that the Kingdom of God has come, that the time is now to begin to live in that state of freedom and detachment toward the mundane symbols of immortality which the path of denial tenders, and to allow the creative, transcending and loving works of the human soul and spirit to prosper. As the ancient God Yahweh placed the choice in front of the Hebrew people, so Jesus placed the choice in front of his contemporaries. The Kingdom of God is among you already if you would only reach out, grasp it and live accordingly!

The radical nature of Jesus' message is most clearly seen in his attitude toward those mundane symbols of immortality which, tendered by the path of denial, were current among his people.

One of these was the perennial symbol of wealth. Wealth has always had a daemonic lure for human beings. Throughout much of the history of our species, survival has been a very real struggle against scarcity. Material prosperity, therefore, is easily transformed into a symbol meaning "more life." The accumulation of wealth becomes a symbol of immortality, a denial of death (scarcity), because it carries the psychic signification of accumulating "more life."

Jesus was very harsh on those who pursued the accumulation of more than was needed to ensure survival.[7] Drawing on the construct of God as a God of justice, as having a moral attitude of partisanship toward the poor and the oppressed, Jesus insisted over and over again that the accumulation of more than one needs to survive is in fact to steal from and exploit those who do not have enough to survive. Wealth stands directly between the rich and their living in the Kingdom of God. The love and pursuit of wealth perverts without exception the creative, transcending and loving works of the soul and spirit. It destroys communion between people and assigns a kind of "monetary value" even to those aspects of human relationships which are most precious to the spirit.

Jesus encouraged us to give and give generously, out of the creative, transcending and loving abundance of a soul and spirit in communion with God. Such generous giving does not think of what "returns" will come from the gift, as if the decision to give or not to give were a result of figures on a balance sheet. It is reported repeatedly that among those wealthy people who did understand and believe the message of Jesus, their first act was to give generously to the poor.

Jesus certainly recognized that maintenance of the physical body is a prerequisite to allowing the creative, transcending and loving works of the soul and spirit to prosper. Just as the pursuit of wealth as an immortality project results in the soul and spirit's perversion, so can the fanatical pursuit of asceticism pervert. Jesus and his circle ate and drank and enjoyed the pleasures of material abundance. Their reaction to the perversions of wealth was not to demand an equal perversion in the opposite direction. Rather, Jesus' teachings show that he strived to enjoy material abundance, having enough, and at the same time maintaining a tentative and detached attitude toward it. That toward which we are to strive is satisfaction with what we have. We need to recognize that "abundance" does not mean ever more and more, but rather it means that we have enough. We are to consider the sparrow, the lilies of the field. They have all that they need for each day and do not strive to accumulate more. They have intrinsic beauty without striving to clothe themselves with ever more symbols of prosperity. Our mother the earth is a good place to live, a gift of God the Creator, and will yield her fruits plentifully for our survival. If we are content with what we have, the earth is a generous provider.

Because of its ancient clan system and consciousness of being a "chosen" people, the family and the nation had become for many a symbol of immortality, something which provided the illusion of meaning and security while falling short of God's true Kingdom. In this area as well we find Jesus affirming these institutions, yet holding them to be tentative, a means to a higher end and not an end in itself.

Bearing children, passing life on to the next generation is a universal symbol of immortality. We all well understand the dictum that "we live on through our children." As an expression of responsibility in this generation for future generations, this is a very positive human emotion.[8] However, the natural desire to procreate as a project of immortality, as a focus for personal meaning in isolation from higher purposes, can easily pervert the creative, transcending and loving works of the soul and spirit. Our children become objects, symbolizing "more life" for ourselves. Children come to be seen as having merit only for their "use value," something to take care of us in our old age. Children come to be seen only as extensions of our own personality. We expect them to "measure up" to our expectations and we experience very personal disappointment if they follow a path different from that which we project for them. We begin to violate their sense of dignity and worth by transforming the responsiblity of parenting, of assisting them in the process of socialization, into attempts to meddle and dictate. In the worst case, our children become status symbols for us, signs of our own wealth and potency.

The family is a wonderful thing. The love and mutuality, closeness and relationships, between marital partners, siblings, parents and children, are certainly gifts of the Creator God. Jesus always affirmed this and seems himself to have had a special kind of love for children, going out of his way to interact with them. However, he demonstrated his attitude of detachment toward the family institution by his decision not to procreate himself. Rather, he sought that kind of closeness and relationship with those of his circle, regardless of their biological connection to him. The love and intimacy among family members is very good. But Jesus seems to be telling us that it cannot stop there. The love which characterizes family relations at their best should be extended beyond the biological unit. Furthermore, when his biological family appeared ready to interfer with his pursuit of God's Kingdom, imposing their sense of proper socialization upon him, Jesus did not hesitate to rebuke them and even temporarily disown them.

Likewise, Jesus never disowned nor depreciated his status as a Hebrew and even saw his mission as being first and foremost to the Jews. The nation or ethnic group might well be a next step in the process of extending "family" love and a sense of mutual aid and

responsibility beyond the biololgical unit. It is very positive to
have this sense of belonging and identity with a nation or ethnic
group. But for those who make this the basis for placing themselves above others, Jesus reminded them that "God could raise
up children of Abraham from these stones!" His willingness to
portray in parable a Samaritan in a positive light as opposed to the
Hebrew characters, as well as his willingness to converse as an
equal with the Samaritan woman, indicate that he understood his
status in the national or ethnic group as a means to another end
and not as an end in itself.

The Hebrew Law, with its many proscriptions and admonitions,
is one of the greatest examples we have of a codification of
communal values in all of history. This Law, with its strong sense
of justice, mutual responsibility and serious attention to duty, has
been a light to all people in the Western world and beyond. But
again, where the Law had become an end in and of itself, Jesus,
the Pharisee of love, felt compelled to debunk this immortality
project. This is not to say that Jesus broke the Law, and even still
less that he "abolished" it. He understood his attitude and actions
as a fulfillment of the law. That is, he saw the Law as a means to an
end, the inauguration of God's Kingdom, rather than as an end in
itself.

Jesus respected the Law as an expression of positive communal
values. But at the same time he strongly insisted that treating the
Law as an end in itself would stifle the environment of freedom
which allows the creative, transcending and loving works of the
soul and spirit to prosper. In such cases Jesus was quick to call
attention to the *intent* of the Law, even going so far as to remind
his people that "Sabbath was made for people. People were not
made for the Sabbath!"

A final area in which Jesus confronted the symbols of immortality
which pervert the works of the soul and spirit was in his relation to
political power.[9] We find this typified in three sorts of encounters.
The first of these was with the occupying Romans.

The Roman state represented the most tangible evidence there
was in the Mediterranean world that the hierarchical political
structures of humankind offer to us the sense of permanence and
solidity for which our hearts long. If ever there was a viable

immortality symbol embodied in the state with which one could identify and melt into in the sense of security of participation in a "higher power," this was it!

Yet we see Jesus' attitude toward the Roman state to be a unique combination of total disrespect and disregard for the state as an institution and a respect born of love for individual people who happened to be representatives of the Roman occupation.

Jesus was more than willing to heal the daughter of the Roman centurion, and even used the faith of this centurion as an example to his followers. Likewise, he advised his followers to go "even yet another mile" for those Roman soldiers who demanded of the people that they carry the soldiers' pack for one mile.

But his attitude toward the Roman state itself was something different altogether. He openly satirized the claims of the Roman rulers to be "benefactors" of the people. He ironically taught that only those whose loyalties were already with the Roman state owed that state anything, while those whose strivings were toward the things of God, toward the creative, transcending and loving works of the soul and spirit, owed that state nothing at all. In his responses to Pontius Pilatus, the Roman governor, Jesus showed no disrespect for Pilatus as a man, yet he made it very clear that any power Pilatus might feel he had over Jesus was an illusion. We have no record that Jesus, unlike many other Hebrews in different times and places, had to face the question directly of having to pay a sign of respect for the Roman emperor as a god. But we must conclude that he would have rejected this forthrightly.

A second place where Jesus confronted political power was in his encounter with Herod and the Herodians. Herod was a kind of puppet king which the Roman state would tolerate in the suzerain nations of the empire. The Herodians were a sort of fading Jewish aristocracy. These were the people who, among the Jews, had totally sold themselves to the Roman state in exchange for the privilege of maintaining certain of the outward trappings of wealth and power. Jesus seems to have had more respect for the Romans than for these people. He called Herod a "fox" and showed nothing but contempt for the Herodians. However, we must be cautious about inferring too much about Jesus' attitudes toward them because his interaction with this group was minimal. He mainly interacted with his own kind, the common people and Pharisaic teachers.

A final place where Jesus confronted political power was in his relations with the Zealot movement.[10] The Zealots were a terrorist force of national liberation. Their goal was to throw out the Roman oppressors and to establish an independent state of Israel. There are heated debates among scholars as to Jesus' attitude toward the Zealots, and it is a difficult problem to sort out. It is made more difficult because it is inevitably colored by our own attitudes toward national liberation movements in the present.

The biblical record reflects the teaching of the early church on this issue. We know that the Palestinian Christians did not participate in the defense of Jerusalem during the uprisings against the Romans in the generation after Jesus, and we must assume this was justified in their view by way of reference to the memory of Jesus' teaching. On the other hand, given Jesus' attitude of opposition toward the Roman state, the fact that his circle of closest disciples did include people who were directly identified as Zealots, and the fact that Jesus himself was martyred by crucifixion, a form of punishment the Romans reserved for political rebels, it is impossible to conclude that Jesus held no common ground with the Zealots.

From a secular point of view it is very difficult to understand what the Zealots were trying to accomplish. With no other weapons than fists, iron wills and the occasional concealed dagger, they took on the power and glory of the entire Roman empire! Did they really think that by ambushing single and drunken Roman soldiers in the night they would wear down the will of the Roman occupation? If so, they simply had no understanding of the kind of human sacrifice a colossal immortality symbol like the Roman empire could chew up and spit out. Like the superpowers of our own day, the more human lives spent in the defense and expansion of the empire, the "more life" that immortality project contained. It literally fed on the spent blood of its citizens and soldiers.

The only way to understand the Zealot actions is in the context of apocalyptic. In this context, the Zealots thought that if they could begin a popular uprising against the Romans, though collective suicide by secular standards, it would provoke the cosmic forces to intervene on the side of the Hebrews. This made much sense in a Hebrew context, for even the great traditions of military victories among them often began with the Hebrew military leader purposely *weakening* his army, sending many of the volunteers home, rejecting the use of iron chariots, and so forth, before going out to meet the opposing armies.[11] Apocalyptic expectations were strong among the social groups with whom Jesus was associated, and there is every reason to believe that Jesus himself shared in much of this apocalyptic sentiment.

On the other hand, Jesus' clear teaching on love for the enemy, his comments on those who would "take the Kingdom by storm," and the fact that the generation of Christians immediately following Jesus distanced themselves unambiguously from the Zealots, are all evidence that Jesus did not simply acquiesce to the Zealot vision.

Jesus never denied that the Kingdom of God he preached was a movement of national liberation. The Roman occupation certainly perceived it to be just that. But was this liberation a goal in itself, and therefore an immortality symbol, or would national liberation be a possible byproduct of living the Kingdom of God now? What is clear is that Jesus did not see an independent state in Palestine as coterminous with the Kingdom of God. His concept of the Kingdom was that it was of a completely different order from the kingdoms and empires of this world. His Kingdom was "not of this world;" it was seen as already "among you and within you." One cannot but respect those who, with total dedication, stand up against a colossal power like the Roman empire. To see the nakedness of that great immortality project and act to oppose it is quite an accomplishment. However, if one opposes such a structure in the name of another project which is less than the Kingdom of God, the "good" which follows will be shortlived, since new perversions of the work of the soul and spirit will follow immediately.

As the poet said:

> To fight, perchance to win! Aye, there's the rub!
> For victory brings privilege and prestige
> And the children of the children of the fighters
> Take it all for granted
> And in turn oppress.

Jesus had respect and sympathy for the Zealots. He clearly taught that God was partisan in favor of those oppressed. But he pointed back to the tradition of the immediate kingship of God, now constructed in the image of a loving parent, as the source for liberation. In spite of the oppressors' claims to glory, we have resources within us already to build that environment of freedom within which the creative, transcending and loving works of the human soul and spirit may prosper. The true and pure soul and spirit does not provoke one to hatred and violence. It rather prods us to recognize, respect and love the humanity, the image of God, in even the enemy, the oppressor. This is not simply an admonition to passive acceptance of oppression. Any comfort the oppressor takes in the "nonviolence" of those oppressed, but who are filled with this spirit, is illusionary.

This is rather a challenge, a calling, for us to tap into that source of dignity and strength which will empower us, as Gandhi and Martin Luther King saw, to continue to return good for evil, to keep loving the enemy until that enemy simply cannot continue in the false mode of perception of his or her immortality project. When violence opposes violence, humankind simply spins its historical wheels. History moves forward, toward a true consummation of the Kingdom of God, toward a full consummation of that environment of freedom within which the creative, transcending and loving works of the human soul and spirit may prosper, only when evil is overcome by good.

Here we have examined Jesus' attitude toward various symbols of immortality which the path of denial tendered for his contemporaries. In each case we have seen that he chose to reject these as projects unworthy of the Kingdom of God. His perspective was informed by a construct of God not as the exacting tyrant mediated through hierarchical structures of power, an unforgiving Judge whose justice demanded fulfillment of minute proscriptions of the Law. He experienced God as a loving parent, the one closest to us, the one who enables us to live and act according to the fruits of creativity, transcendence and love, which are the works of the human soul and spirit.

To those who have chosen the path of denial, of opting for a life goal which falls short of the Kingdom of God – wealth, servility to the Law, national chauvinism, subservience to or armed resistance against the Roman state – Jesus had but one message. "You must be born again!" *Metanoiete!* You must change your values. You must leave the path of denial and come into the Kingdom of freedom. You must come to a new construct of the image of God.

This is the teaching of that man to whom our faith points as the incarnation of God in human history.

5

Toward a
Critical Christology

Jesus of Nazareth came teaching a new message to his contemporaries, that the Kingdom of God was at hand, that all we need do to enter that Kingdom was to believe in its possibility and to live accordingly. To live according to this new Kingdom meant to forsake the values which systems of unfreedom thrust upon us and to value instead human community, mutuality and trust. The idols of our immortality projects destroy human community, mutuality and trust, binding us in systems of unfreedom. In answer to the human predicament, Jesus, the Pharisee of love, preached a new construct of God based on the model of a loving parent. In the value system generated by this view of God, the "least of these" are primarily treasured. The one who would be the greatest should become the servant of all. The first shall be last and the last shall be first. It was, in short, an ironic reversal of the value systems of unfreedom.

Jesus' teachings as we have had them handed down to us are neither systematic nor exhaustive. It is clear that a very large part of the impact he had on his followers had not so much to do with his teachings *per se*, but with his personality, life and example. Around Jesus, many of his followers caught a glimpse of what life in that Kingdom of God, that kingdom of freedom, where the creative, transcending and loving works of the soul and spirit are nurtured and prosper, was like. As with our own experience today, a central place where that new perception became a reality was eating at table. The legends of the tradition go so far as to say that two of his circle did not even recognize Jesus until they sat down to eat with him.

Jesus was killed, murdered by the Roman occupation forces. This was a stark reminder to his followers that this new kingdom of freedom would be perceived as a mortal threat to those whose values were formed by the systems of oppression. It was a very frightening lesson and the tradition says that, at least initially, his circle of followers scattered in fear.

Yet the experience of the Kingdom of God which they had had in their association with Jesus proved stronger than their fear. Exactly how it happened remains something of a mystery. But the vision these followers caught from Jesus lived on in them after Jesus' death. They regrouped and, now with a fervor of genuine conviction, began to spread the good news of God's Kingdom themselves. Because of them, in the words of Willi Marxsen, "die Sache Jesu geht weiter!" The cause of Jesus lives on![1]

Jesus' closest followers, probably following the lead of Simon Peter, began to preach that Jesus, although murdered by the Roman occupation forces, had been raised to new life by God. Jesus, they now taught, had in fact been the promised Messiah, the anointed one, who brought in the Kingdom of God. Dying and being raised to new life became a powerful metaphor for the call to become part of the Jesus movement, those who were living the Kingdom of God already. These people began to refer to Jesus with honorific titles, such as Lord and King, which Jesus had abjured during his own lifetime.[2]

It is now well established among scholars that in his preaching, Jesus did not point to himself but rather to God as the proper focus for religious devotion.[3] Yet we find in the earliest strata of Christian documents, such as the first epistle of Paul to the church in Thessalonica, a dual focus on both "God the Father and the Lord Jesus Christ." In other words, from the earliest times of which we have record, the religion *of* Jesus was beginning to be turning into a religion *about* Jesus.[4] There are parallels to this in other religions as well – for example, in Buddhism. We are left to deal with this development as we, the heirs of the Christian tradition, try to make sense religiously in our own time.

Jesus pointed to a construct of God based on the model of a loving parent. The church increasingly focused on Jesus, trans-forming him first into the eschatological Messiah who would return, then the Lord and Christ who was already reigning in heaven with God, and finally a person in Godself. Jesus was deified.

If we remember that the religious urge is inextricably bound to the human quest for meaning, we can sympathize with those who, in stages, deified Jesus. Their own sense of meaning and purpose could not be separated from their hope for an eschatological redeemer or from that taste of the Kingdom of God which they experienced in communities gathered in the name of Jesus. As they struggled to construct an image of God which would reflect the sense of meaning and purpose they had, it followed that Jesus would begin to play a crucial and central role in that new construction. God symbolized their greatest hopes and Jesus was the center of those hopes. Each community of "Jesus people" constructed new ways of articulating that fact.

Among the earliest Christians, Aramaic Jews in Palestine, Jesus was seen as having been appointed by God as the apocalyptic Son of Man who would finally bring an end to history. Jesus taught what has been called a "present-future" view of God's Kingdom.[5] This was carried on in the table fellowship of the Aramaic Jews who were followers of Jesus. But already in ascribing the role of the Son of Man to Jesus, there was a subtle shift in emphasis occurring whereby it was possible to distinguish between the present and future in God's Kingdom. They thought that Jesus would return in his role of the Danielic Son of Man even in their lifetime, topple the mighty and bring an end to human history (cf. Daniel 7:13ff.).

The Greek-speaking Jews who were also followers of Jesus agreed that Jesus would play the role of the returning apocalyptic Son of Man. But they added to the earlier constructions the idea that, as the Christ, Jesus already was ruling in heaven during the interim before his return. Here we see a new emphasis on an ontological teaching about Jesus, not only the functional teaching of the Aramaic community. Finally, as the Jesus movement spilled over into the Gentile world, Gentile converts began to picture Jesus in purely ontological terms, as the pre-existent Son of God, the Logos, who briefly came to earth and then returned to heaven after his death.

It would be too easy to fault these early Christians for this transformation in their teachings about Jesus. However, it must also be remembered that they often found themselves in situations of extremity. As the Roman empire began to collapse, many of its rulers became increasingly tyrannical and drunk with their own sense of invincibility. Many made demands that they be worshipped as divine beings themselves. This demand the early Christians had to refuse. Yet on what basis could they stand up to the Roman Emperor, the most powerful person on earth at that time? The more power and glory the Caesar claimed for himself, the more power and glory the church claimed for Jesus as an antidote. If we remember that the claim the "Jesus is Lord!" had as its correlative "Caesar is *not* Lord!", we can understand and sympathize with the deifers of Jesus. It was a powerful survival strategy.[6]

Sympathy with the process of the deification of Jesus does not, however, mean uncritical acceptance. The fact is that this entire tradition has become very problematic for intelligent Christians since at least the seventeenth century. During the so-called Enlightenment, thoughtful Christians first began to feel uncomfortable with "miracle" stories in the Bible, since this appeared to cast a long shadow of primitive superstition over the narratives. However, even during the Enlightenment period it was never seriously questioned that there do indeed exist transcendent universals which can be objectively known, either through reason or revelation. Yet this is exactly what our contemporary situation of pluralism and post-Enlightenment historical consciousness has forced us to question deeply. Therefore, in our time the problems we have with the entire tradition of an ontological Godman have become acute and have left many of us wondering what, if anything, all of this could possibly mean to us.

It is impossible, both on intellectual and moral grounds, to continue to expect an apocalyptic end to human history, unless it be one of our own making. We can no longer see God as a Being who stands apart from the natural order and intervenes at will in that order. Our quest for a sense of meaning and purpose now takes place in radically new circumstances compared with those of the early Christians – or medieval and later Christians, for that matter. We now know that we and we alone must write the next chapter of human history. We cannot depend on an apocalyptic Son of Man or any other force to step in from outside human history to save us should we continue in our march toward collective suicide. If the metaphor of Incarnation can mean anything at all in our time, it can only point us to the historical relativity of even our notions of God. It points to the radical responsibility for our future which this lays on our shoulders.

In as much as the deified Christ has simply become one more immortality symbol in whose service people are killed, marginalized and kept in bondage to systems of oppression, we must be willing to let that deified Christ go. We must take a stand of unbelief toward that Christ. In as much as a deified Christ allows us to escape responsibility in a posture of resignation or passivity toward oppression and our march toward collective suicide, we must be willing to let that deified Christ go. We must take a stand of unbelief toward that Christ. In as much as a deified Christ has become a symbol under which to conquer, we must be willing to let that deified Christ go. We must take a stand of unbelief toward that Christ. In as much as a deified Christ divides us from our brothers and sisters of other religious traditions, we must be willing to let that deified Christ go. We must take a stand of unbelief toward that Christ. In as much as a deified Christ confirms us in our prejudices of race, religion, class, sex and sexual orientation, we must be willing to let that deified Christ go. We must take a stand of unbelief toward that Christ.

We have no choice but to be critical of the Christian tradition. Just as we must assume ethical responsibility for our construct of God, so must we also assume ethical responsibility for our teaching about Christ.[7] For Christians, the two are inseparable.

On what, therefore, might we base a positive christology for our time? I would offer the following points for further exploration.[8]

We know by experience that life is not reducible to either the material or the nonmaterial. We must reject, therefore, any attempt to present ultimate reality, ultimate concern, as either mental or material activity. Any experience of life includes both the material and mental/spiritual aspects. We experience the unity of the material and mental/spiritual aspects of our being most concretely in our relationship to ourselves and other people. Therefore, we can best express our ideas about ultimate reality, ultimate concern, by employing personal metaphors.

This sense of unity is felt most strongly in relationships of love. Love respects the independence of the other as a personality and resists in relation to the loved one those value systems which would divide or fragment the loved one. Therefore, as we employ personal metaphors to express our experience of ultimate reality, ultimate concern, we do well to relate those metaphors as closely as possible to the concept of love.

In employing personal metaphors closely related to the concept of love to express our experience of ultimate reality, ultimate concern, it is no longer possible to hold nonpersonal institutions, such as, especially, the state, as the locus of highest moral authority. Moral authority springs only from the creative, transcending and loving promptings of the soul and spirit.

Christians may well find the personal metaphors of the christological tradition useful and meaningful. If so, we are free to employ them. But we are not compelled to do so. As this relates to christological language, we may well find that titles such as friend, helper, teacher and sibling (brother) are better metaphors than those which come from relations of hierarchy (Lord, Master, King). It may be that for certain terms which are heavily laden with hierarchical overtones, it would be best to call a moratorium on their use for the time being. This is not something which can be proscribed by theologians. Theologians must, rather, be attentive to those metaphors which are used and those which are neglected among the least powerful sectors of the community and use that as a guide in their constructive work.[9]

As much as is possible, we must reverse the process of exchanging the religion of Jesus for a religion about Jesus. Jesus pointed toward the direct experience of the Kingdom of God in the present-future. It was certainly not his intention that his message of the presence of God's Kingdom of freedom should devolve into yet another form of religion. We cannot simply change the fact that that is what happened. We need not "abandon" the Christian religion any more than Jesus abandoned Judaism. It is our religious tradition, and in spite of its faults has proven power to motivate love and concern among its followers.

Nevertheless, we can see clearly the manner in which the early church shifted the message of Jesus. The church hypostatized the present-future Kingdom which Jesus proclaimed, identifying it with Jesus himself. By use of first functional and then ontological christologies, the church reduced the Kingdom of God to one man.[10] Jesus invited all of us into God's Kingdom of freedom. But once the Kingdom became focused on one man, the gate was effectively closed to the rest of us, at least in this life. The promise of heaven in the next life is scant replacement for Jesus' invitation into the Kingdom in the present-future. We must reclaim from Christian tradition our invitation to enter that Kingdom now.[11]

This led directly to a second shift the church affected in the message of Jesus. Jesus focused his attention on the present future, a radically prophetic view of time. But once the church began to focus on Jesus rather than on the Kingdom Jesus proclaimed as the locus for meaning and purpose, it was inevitable that his view of time would be replaced with a scheme of salvation history in which Jesus became the "center" of history.[12] In this scheme, the present loses all significance, except as a veil of tears through which one must pass on the way from the "past" salvation worked by Christ to the "future" salvation worked by Christ. This had a particularly detrimental effect on Christian ethics. For whereas in Jesus' teachings, the promise of eschatology was translated into the demand for spontaneous acts of justice, love and mercy, in the new scheme, only the "works of the church," those prescribed rituals designed to get us through this insignificant present, could be valued.[13] Jesus' message that the future is already present, that forgiveness, grace and mercy are everywhere in the liberating practice of love, that God had taken presence in the people, was first obscured and then lost in christological formulae of a preexistent, incarnate and then exalted Son of God.

The early Christians assigned titles and offices to Jesus Christ in an attempt to express what it was about this man which was unique, different from other human beings, for them. It was their attempt to express that special quality which they experienced when gathered for table fellowship in Jesus' name. Is Jesus still unique for us today? Or to put the question in its traditional form, "Is there salvation outside of Christ?"

This is a difficult question to answer because it assumes an intimate experience of other religious traditions. It should be referred to those who have such an intimate experience. As far as I understand it, there appears to be a great similarity between Jesus and the Buddha, not only in the fact that both pointed to the freedom of living in the present-future, but also in terms of the way the followers of both these men magnified their teacher after his death.

Jesus' ethical teachings have parallels in all of the great religious traditions, and all of his teachings can also be found in the rabbinical sources of his contempories.[14] Even his vision of God's Kingdom of freedom in the present-future has also been taught by other great religious figures: the Buddha, Francis of Assisi, the Baal Shem Tov, Martin Buber and many others.

Of course Jesus was unique in the sense that all individuals are unique. Jesus stood in a particular historical communal tradition. Because of this, Jesus was tempted by similar paths of denial which we face today as well – accumulation of wealth, deification of the state, the family, ethnic group and its communal law code. In each of these cases, as was seen, his attitude to these symbols of immorality remains instructive for us today.

On the other hand, no matter what titles and offices of honour we ascribe to Jesus, when we face some of the great ethical questions of our day – biomedical issues, family and sexual issues, the arms race, global economic issues – we simply draw a blank from Jesus' teachings. At most we can find there some general principles which we must then interpret and apply. But we are most likely to do this completely out of context, and in any case, these are then our interpretations and applications, not those of Jesus.

The point is, no matter how magnificent the language we employ in our christological formulae, it is impossible to "follow Jesus" as some new kind of code. He simply had nothing directly to say on many of the most pressing issues of our day. We are left to follow our own best prompting of the soul and spirit on these things, whether we picture Jesus as a human prophet who lived and died, or as the pre-existent Son of God who reigns in heaven sitting on the right hand of the Father. And we are more likely to remain humble with our interpretations and applications within the context of the former construct.

What we do have is Jesus' promise that if we "seek first the Kingdom of God," that is, if we genuinely listen to the creative, transcending and loving promptings of the soul and spirit and determine as much as possible to live in the present-future of the kingdom of freedom, then "all the rest will be given to you." But again, this promise is made credible not because it was given by an ontological Godman. It is made credible in the actual experience of those who strive to be in tune with the creative, transcending and loving promptings of the soul and spirit.[15]

The question of the uniqueness of Christ has traditionally been expressed in the question, "Is there salvation outside of Christ?" In our time, as we stand in solidarity with the victims of Christian antisemitism, with our native American brothers and sisters whose genes still carry the effects of smallpox purposely inflicted on them by Christians, with our once enslaved black brothers and sisters, with the victims of economic and cultural imperialism, with people marginalized by sexism and homophobia, the question is reversed. "Can one still find salvation in Christ?"[16] Our christological reflections cannot escape or ignore this new consciousness. We believe that one can find salvation, meaning and purpose in Christ. But not in those Christs who presided over and justified such marginalization and murder.

The entire urgency of the question of the uniqueness of Christ arises only for those who have made some particular "Christ" into an immortality project of denial. Only then does one percieve as a threat recognition of the same truth from other sources. Those who have experienced the present-future kingdom of freedom and mutuality at table fellowship with those of other belief systems are not likely to feel much urgency in defending the uniqueness of their Christ.

Nevertheless, for Christians, the God they find in the deepest levels of their soul and spirit will likely continue to wear the face of Jesus. What we affirm about Christ is inseparable from what we affirm about God and, ultimately, about our own lives. If grasping that present-future kingdom of love and freedom is still an option for us, fidelity and Christian faith obligates us to reach out for it, even if that means demythologizing and even abandoning entirely pre-existent/incarnate/exalted christological language. After all, that is what Jesus would have done.

6

Church Without Dogma

The church formed and progressed through human history with a
strong conviction that God exists in an objective sense, outside
and above human history; that God called the church into being
and directs the church in a special and particular unity. Does not
the approach to religious thinking employed here destroy that
unity? Does not the original hypothesis with which we began,
since it moves interpretation away from transcendent categories
altogether, exclude *a priori* the objective basis for unity? If, in
thinking religiously, we construct our own images of God which
are not intended to be statements of description in relation to an
object, does this not take constructive pluralism over the line into
destructive relativism?

There is no doubt that the ecclesia, the gathered group, will
ground itself in unity in a different way from what has been the
case until now, as people of faith begin to work out new paradigms
for understanding and interpreting their life together. This does
not mean, however, that constructive pluralism among people of
faith must degenerate into destructive relativism. It is, rather, a
necessary adjustment to the intellectual and social situation in
which people of faith find themselves in our society.

Beginning at least with the sixteenth century, the church as an
institutional power has been on the decline. Speaking of the time
before the Protestant split, it is more or less possible to speak of
"the church," although this betrays a decidedly Eurocentric perspective. It is impossible to speak that way of the past five hundred
years of history. At an increasing rate, "the church" is becoming a
meaningless abstraction. What we must speak of are many and

diverse churches. These churches do not speak or respond in unity on even one of the major issues of our day. A profile of how these churches do respond to the great issues of our day would likely parallel closely the responses of society generally, reflecting the same attitudes of class and race, in spite of any claims of "guidance" from a transcendent source. The function of this claim to guidance from a transcendent source is simply to confirm people in their prejudices, to mask and obscure the social and political sources of these prejudices, and to cut off further discussion of the issues involved.

Therefore, an approach to religious thought which does not assume a transcendent source of guidance, but instead strives to make explicit its social and political vision as the basis for communal gathering of people of faith does not *create* disunity among the churches. It begins with the fact of disunity and attempts to think religiously within that context.

The churches have historically sought unity on the basis of the language they employ – that is, a unity of creed and doctrine. In many ancient cultures, but particularly in the cultures out of which the churches arose, speech was seen as a particularly powerful act, and the "Word" was viewed in a magical context. To name an object gave power over that object, and naming of children was a particularly significant act. It was assumed that the child would acquire traits which were contained in the name itself. Therefore, it is quite clear why so much stress would be placed in the past on "correct" verbal formulations of religious truth.

Modern linguistic theories also stress the importance of language in shaping social reality. There is perhaps no absolutely prelingual experience of reality. If such an experience of reality were possible, it would nevertheless be impossible to describe. The power of language does not reside in the words themselves, but in language as an integral component of a complex social and cultural experience which must be learned. Through language the person learns the social codes which convey the meaning which social experience has for other people. Through language a person communicates to others his or her own cultural experience and so learns to situate himself or herself in the cultural environment. Learning the correct use of language is the most important part of the process of socialization. It is through a common use of language that people communicate. Therefore, while there may be no prelingual experience of reality, the developed communication process does assume prior, common cultural experience. Interlocutors must have learned to use language in compatible ways for the communication process to take place.

The most basic experiences are common to all people. "I am hungry" requires no more than a literal translation of the words into a tongue common to the interlocutors for communication to take place. As concepts become more abstract, however, literal translations become increasingly unsatisfactory. Dictionaries can easily be programmed into computers. Yet translations of even simple business letters produced by this method are unintelligible unless closely controlled by one who has command of all languages involved in the translation. This is painfully obvious to anyone who has tried to assemble a child's toy on Christmas morning following instructions produced by literal translation!

To learn a foreign language, grammar books are helpful only up to a certain point, beyond which the learner must be immersed in the history and literature of the people who speak the language. One must share in the cultural experience of the people, seeing life the way they do on a level at which the cultural meaning of the words employed are formed.[1]

A common experience of life is necessary for communication between people. Words and symbols[2] employed in the communication process in turn shape a person's own experience of life. Language is the tool of a dialogue process between a person's internal and external experience of reality. Therefore, some internal experience of reality is logically prior to the communication process. Through language, a person tests his or her own experience of reality with that of other people and assimilates other people's experience of reality into his or her own interpretations.

In normal circumstances we take the communication process for granted, for life goes on in stable fashion. Most often, we share a common cultural experience with those with whom we come into contact. Communication in everyday life proceeds at such low levels of abstraction that even newcomers can pick up the necessary background of experience rather quickly. Yet our humor is full of situations in which there is a snag in the communication process. An American and a English person do the same thing in response to the command to "fasten seat belts." But these same two might do something quite different in response to the command to "remove your bonnets."

While such situations cause momentary embarrassment, we have a well-established method for sorting out the difficulty. We point to the object designated by a particular word. So long as *actions* correspond, we are justified in assuming that valid communication has taken place. When our actions do not correspond, we know we must retrace and sort out the difficulty.

This point is made clear by Anatol Rapoport in his book *Operational Philosophy.*[3] There it is demonstrated why the language of natural science has been so fruitful. Discourse in the natural sciences has proceeded by way of agreed methods for sorting out any snags that occur in the communication process. This is most easy when there is a concrete object to which one can point. But this is not always the case, even in the natural sciences. In such cases, says Rapoport, scientists must employ an "extensional bargain."[4] Agreement that communication has taken place is based on observing common actions among the communicators. The higher the level of abstraction – the further away interlocutors get from objects to which they can point – the more an extensional bargain must be relied upon.

Discussions of such high abstraction were passed off by logical positivism as "nonsense." That kind of strident, anti-clerical atheism seemed good and down-to-earth when directed against the metaphysicians of religious thought. But what if the same analysis would silence the conversations of theoretical physicists? At very high levels of abstraction – where there does not exist an object to which one can point – extensional bargains are necessary and unavoidable if valid communication is to proceed.

The categories employed in religious thought are among the most abstract concepts in human language. Religious thought takes as its primary subject-matter the immediate experience of reality. In religious thought, the discourse with which people attempt to communicate their experience of faith with others, frequent and conscious use of extensional bargains must be expected. Yet this is exactly what is curtailed when a unity of language, of a common creed or doctrine, is made the basis for unity among people of faith. Relativism on the level of language is becoming increasingly the norm for religious discourse. If communication is to proceed on course, it is necessary that we make corresponding actions, a corresponding ethical stance toward the world, the basis for unity.

A person's moral and ethical stance toward the world is a more accurate indicator of the spiritual state of that person than is the language employed by that person to communicate his or her spiritual state.[5] A spiritual life of fear and mistrust, of the path of denial, will be made public in actions. A spiritual life of love and trust, of the path of acceptance, will be made public in actions.

A unity based on the language employed to communicate spiritual life may or may not constitute a unity of spiritual life among a people of faith. If we assume that a spiritual life of love and trust, of the path of acceptance, will issue in an ethical stance toward the world most broadly characterized as pacifist[6] and that a spiritual life of fear and mistrust, of the path of denial, will issue in an ethical stance toward the world most broadly characterized as nonpacifist, then we may see this issue as a watershed in determining the spiritual state of the person. Here it is clear that those churches which base their unity on a common creed or doctrine divide internally on exactly this issue. That such a division exists and will continue to exist is, in fact, the official position of these churches. The stand one takes in relation to, for example, military service, which is a very good indicator of a given church's teaching on love of the enemy, is considered an accidental, not an essential, of the Christian faith. We must assume, therefore, that a unity based on common creed of doctrine is not a good indicator of unity of the spirit.

A unity among people of faith based on an observable common moral and ethical stance toward the world is a more adequate basis for assuming a unity of the spirit. To the exent that a unity of the spirit is desirable among the gathered people of faith, we must assume that an ethical unity is more adequate than is common consent to a particular creed or doctrine.

Unity based on a common ethical stance toward the world requires frequent and conscious striking of extensional bargains. When agreement is not found on the level of language, we must then proceed on the basis of shared ethical concern, mindful and respectful that each person's "way of saying it" is one fallible attempt to express in words a common and shared spiritual experience.

Words and symbols are tools employed to express a person's spiritual condition and experience. These words and symbols, in turn, shape the spiritual life of each person. How particular words and symbols are assimilated by each person depends on the particularities of individual biography. Because individual biographies are personal, it cannot be assumed that words and symbols used to communicate a person's spiritual condition will be employed or understood in the same way by each person, even among people who are part of the same national culture. The language and symbols chosen by each person may differ significantly from one person to another. But we can respect the integrity of each variant expression because of the deeper commonality, pointing toward a unity of the spirit, which we see on the level of ethical commitment.

Let us take as one illustration two people who employ directly contradictory language in relation to the symbol of God. One says that God exists. The other insists that God does not exist. Clearly, on the level of language, there is no common ground here. But each continues to assume a unity of the spirit because each recognizes in the other a common ethical stance toward the world. Each sees that the other encounters the world in terms of trust and love. So long as each recognizes this in the other, an extensional bargain of agreement can be struck on the level of language.

What does the one mean by the statement "God exists," and the other by the statement "God does not exist?" For the sake of illustration, let us grossly simplify the nexus of human experience. One person was brought up in a home environment in which parents were kind, loving and trustworthy. For that person, a symbol pointing to divine parenthood expresses that which is kind, loving and trustworthy. Therefore, it comes easily that this symbol of divine parenthood (God) would be employed to express a spiritual experience of the world as trustworthy. It says, in effect, that this world is a world in which the path of acceptance, in which an ethic of trust and love, can be taken with confidence. For God exists!

The other person, on the other hand, has had a very negative experience of parenthood. For such a person, a symbol pointing to divine parenthood only signifies that which is fearful, mistrustful, stifling of creativity. Therefore, he or she finds it very difficult to employ a symbol of divine parenthood to express a spiritual experience of the world as trustworthy and infused with love. In the case of this second person, coming to the conclusion that God does not exist, that the world is not a place in which fear and mistrust create and rule, and that therefore one can live according to the path of acceptance, according to an ethic of love and trust, with full confidence, may be a very valid way of expressing his or her spiritual experience. One may act with confidence and trust in this world because that great tyrant of tyrants in the sky is not real and does not exist!

It is clear that a unity of people of faith based on a common ethical stance toward the world would radically change the structure of most of the churches. It would force the churches to state clearly the kind of ethical stance toward the world they expect of the people of faith, removing the mask of religious ideology which now obscures the social and political situation of the churches. It would also make authoritarian structures within the churches much more difficult to maintain and rationalize. In short, the churches would begin increasingly to resemble enclaves of dissent in the society, as modeled since at least the sixteenth century by groups from the dissenting traditions.

Those raised in dissenting religious traditions have had the language and symbols of the religion passed on to them in ways which do not necessarily carry with them an alignment with an unloving and stifling *status quo*. It may be easier for those within dissenting traditions, therefore, to employ such language and symbols to express a spiritual experience of the world as trustworthy and infused with love. But it cannot be forgotten that for many people the language and symbols of religious tradition have been inverted and express something quite opposite to an experience of the world as trustworthy and infused with love. The cross of Christ, for example, might be a powerful symbol of pacific trust in the power of love. But it is also a symbol under which whole populations have been slaughtered, inquisitions and witch hunting have been carried out, and countless people have been frightened and bullied into social conformity.

It should not be surprising that large numbers of people are seeking to express spiritual experience by employing language and symbols other than those of the Christian tradition. This may take the form of borrowing language and symbols from other religions, or in a stand of principled atheism toward the language and symbols of the Christian religion. Those of dissenting religious traditions may be in the best position to sympathize with, encourage and interact creatively with such developments among people of faith.

In the absence of a dogmatic structure to enforce conformity to creed of doctrine, would total anarchy exist among people of faith in the area related to verbal expressions of spiritual experience? Is it possible to foster and encourage pluralism in the verbal expression of spiritual experience and still take language seriously? Is it really the case that any and all use of language and symbols is of equal value?

Let us return to the illustration I began above. Both people claim a spiritual experience in which trust and love are seen as primary creative and sustaining principles in the world. One expresses that by saying that God exists. The other expresses that by saying that God does not exist. Within a structure of a gathering of people of faith, they contemplate their spiritual experience of the world and in freedom, without fear of censorship, speak to the group of spiritual truth as they see it. It is understood by the group that such attempts to put spiritual experience into words are always experimental and tentative. Likewise, responses from the group are also experimental and tentative.

As spiritual experience is shared in this way, people of faith open up to one another windows to their spiritual life. People begin to understand more completely the biographical context within which each person works to formulate verbal and symbolic expressions of their spiritual experience. As this learning process proceeds, the people in our illustration, who oppose each other so diametrically on the question of the existence of God, begin to understand better what each means by the word "God." Eventually, they might be able to say to each other, "Aha! So *that* is what 'God' means to you. Understanding that, I can see why you would insist that God does (or does not) exist." Both may continue to prefer one formula over another. But both will have reached a higher level of understanding which neither could have reached alone without attempting seriously to understand the position of the other. And that, after all, is at least one of the major goals and benefits of a meeting of people of faith.

There are a number of meeting structures which can facilitate this kind of openness. Certainly one of the best is the silent meeting practiced among Quakers. Meeting for silence could be incorporated into the worship styles of many traditions, as well as other structural forms which facilitate and encourage such openness among the people of faith. Meetings of the gathered people of faith must become free from dogma, allowing freedom of expression, and encouraging experimental approaches to language so that contemplative spiritual life can be nurtured. And unity will not be found in creeds or doctrines, but in basic moral and ethical commitments of the participants. As an increasing number of people are seeking to express their spiritual experience of the world as trustworthy and infused with love in language and symbols other than those of the historic Christian tradition, new models for worship become imperative in the context of mission work and ecumenical discussion.

Doctrinal and credal pluralism coupled with seeking for unity for the gathered people of faith has been presented here as a response to the new intellectual and socio-political situation, in which it has become impossible to view God as a Being outside of human history. Therefore it is also impossible to see our religious thinking as descriptive in the same sense that we employ language to describe other objects. It would be wrong, however, to assume that this approach to unity is itself new and has no historical precedents within Christian history.

The first generation for Christians certainly leaned toward a unity of ethics. This was not only because of the strong influence of the Jewish religion upon the earliest Christians, although that was certainly part of it. The fact is that dogmatic formulae simply did not yet exist among them, nor was there any executive structure among them to enforce orthodoxy. Their gatherings were open to all comers, and biblical and extratestamental literature makes it abundantly clear that doctrinal pluralism was the rule among the early Christians.[7]

Christianity was soon introduced into the Hellenistic environment, in which the political and mystical religions were in a decadent state. There were, to be sure, very creative attempts on the part of Jews in diaspora to interpret Jewish monotheism within the context of the best Hellenistic religious and philosophical categories. And this created some interest among non-Jews. But proselytism in Judaism was a very arduous and complicated matter, demanding, among other things, circumcision of the male. Part of the reason Christianity and not Judaism became the major religion of the Roman world was the fact that Christianity could more easily assimilate opposing mythologies in a plurality of doctrines.

Peter Munz wrote a book more than twenty years ago which has been largely ignored, but which helps us to understand the issues involved in this discussion.[8] Munz argued that there are two main axes in the symbol picture (which he calls mythology). One is that of a "male/creationist" myth of origins. The other is that of a "female/emanantal" myth of origins. By placing the redeemer myth against the symbol picture of creation, we arrive at a metaphysics of Absolute Love, or what Munz characterizes as a metaphysics of "relationship." By placing the redeemer myth against the symbol picture of emanation, we arrive at a metaphysics of Absolute Consciousness, or what Munz characterizes as a metaphysics of "solitude." These are quite different conclusions, yet both can form the basis of a pacifist moral stand toward the world. A metaphysics of relationship, or Absolute Love, leads in the direction of an action-oriented, messianically hopeful ethical stand, in which forgiveness of evil overcomes the need for revenge or punishment because the future, rather than the past, is the all-embracing category. A metaphysics of solitude, or Absolute Consciousness, leads in the direction of a contemplative ethical stand, in which pain and suffering are assimilated and negated in the higher consciousness that "All is One" and therefore without need for assigning blame, for revenge or compensation, for the present is the all-embracing category.

In both of these moral stands toward the world, we finally arrive at an ethic which can be broadly characterized as pacifist. Munz, furthermore, insists that the two approaches are complementary, keeping issues of justice in front of the practitioner of solitude, and relativizing and humbling the messianic pretensions of the practitioner of relationship. The ideal would be to keep these two basic approaches in creative tension with one another. This is the creative tension implied by the view of God's Kingdom as "present-future" oriented. In God's Kingdom the absolute future becomes also the absolute present for those who will grasp it. Yet it is exactly the tendency to split the two apart which takes place when we attempt to find unity in language, in a common creed, set of doctrines, or an authoritarian interpretation of sacred texts. Unity based on a recognized common moral stand toward the world, a unity of ethics, allows us to keep these two perspectives in creative tension.

It has been argued in certain forms of biblical theology and conservative existential theology that the early church did wrong not to insist on an exclusive creationist symbol picture. For by allowing its redeemer myth to be placed against an emanantal symbol picture, Christianity was effectively cut off from its roots in Judaism and finally replaced the God of Abraham, Isaac and Jacob with the "God of the philosophers." It is quite clear that, in terms of ideology, a group seeking its unity in terms of a shared ethical commitment would open the doors wide for all kinds of emanantal symbols as tools of language for expressing spiritual experience. This view surfaces periodically in the form of contemplative "univeralism."[9]

It is difficult to accept the idea that no one symbol picture is more or less true than another, and that each can be used positively. Yet there is evidence enough to question this bias which would force us to choose one or the other.

The witness of the early Christians. The early Christians allowed the story of Jesus' death and resurrection to be preached against the backdrop of various symbol pictures, some creationist and some emanantal. Certainly many anomalies in Christian theology could have been avoided had there been a strict insistence on the male/creationist symbol picture of Jewish orthodoxy. Pluralism gained Christian converts, but also made it possible that Christianity should become the religion of the empire. For by making the present absolute, it was concluded that the "Christian" empire must represent the Kingdom of God. The result was the tragic inversion of Christian ideology, against which we now protest.

On the other hand, had there been a strict adherence to the male/creationist mythology among those who formed a sect within Judaism, insisting that Jesus of Nazareth was the Anointed One, the Messiah, it is doubtful whether the sect would have become anything other than a small and short-lived phenomenon, one among many other competing contemporary Jewish sects.

Furthermore, as Elaine Pagels demonstrated in her work on gnosticism,[10] attempts to control the symbol picture against which Christ could be "authoritatively" preached, were an essential part of the rise of an exclusively male-dominated hierarchy within the church. It is the delegitimization of this hierarchical system of authority within the church which, whether one greets this with joy or regret, is at the root of the delegitimization of Christianity in general which has been taking place since the Enlightenment. This should be taken as a clear warning that attempts to control the symbol picture through which spiritual experience may legitimately be expressed can produce unintended secondary effects in the life of the church which are more destabilizing than constructive pluralism could ever be.

The witness of dissenting radicals such as Anabaptists and Quakers. Dissenting radicals such as Anabaptists and Quakers were, for the most part, rooted firmly in biblical, evangelical theology – that is, the male/creationist frame of reference. Yet there are examples aplenty in which appeals to the authority of the Spirit in each believer, to the Inner Light, and so on, can only with great strain be held within that male/creationist frame of reference. Recent scholarly attention focusing on the element of "mysticism" in the formative period of various dissenting groups has highlighted the fact that both poles in the symbol picture, a metaphysics of relationship and a metaphysics of solitude, were being cultivated simultaneously among them. It might, in fact, be argued that it was exactly when one or the other approach crowded the other out that the dissenting group lost its critical edge and formed yet another sectarian branch of Christian history.

The witness of pacifist mystics. Pacifist mystics are present among all of the world's great religious traditions. Firmly rooted in a metaphysics of solitude, it is hard for those who do not have a mystical bent to understand the religious experience of such mystics. Yet it has been demonstrated in numerous contexts that the example and writings of these mystics, such as Meister Eckhart, have had a profound influence of reformers and radicals who are themselves more action-oriented. There is a preservative effect in the mystical experience of God which gives strength to those whose religious experience can more easily be expressed in terms of the metaphysics of relationship.

The witness of feminism. Feminist sisters have now made explicit the pain and alienation they feel when they are expected to express their own spiritual experience in terms of the dominant male/creationist imagery. Dissenting groups have been far ahead of the Christian churches as a whole in terms of giving women more equal status – although this is done most often rather unconsciously, by lowering the authoritative status of all offices within the group. In any case, the experience of the dissenting groups can be taken as a positive model. Many feminist theologians have been exploring female/emanantal imagery and have placed their fingers on the fact that while male/creationist imagery should lead to an ethics characterized by pacific love, it can and most often has been inverted and led to an ethic of power and domination. This witness needs to be heard. There is a growing need for males and females to work together in dialogue toward common imagery in their religious thinking. This does not mean sameness, but rather mutual respect.

A unity based on shared ethical concern is more adequate to our time for the gathered community than is a unity of creed or set of doctrines, if indeed a unity of the spirit is desired. There are various forms, such as Quaker silent worship and other nonauthoritarian structures, within which this unity of practice could be cultivated. The pitfall of this approach is that it unquestionably elevates pluralism to a level at which we have not had much experience or an established track record. This can be frightening.

On the other hand, syncretic exploration of symbols from various religious and secular traditions is already taking place anyway and will likely continue in the future. The inversion of Christian language and symbols which carry the ordinary meaning of them for most people makes this exploration necessary, and a positive indication that people are seeking to find ways in which they can, with integrity, give expression to their experience of the world as trustworthy and loving. The challenge, therefore, is not to hinder this exploratory process, but rather to build up and enhance structures within which the freedom to explore does not degenerate into unproductive individualism. The emphasis on unity based on shared ethical commitment is one way to keep people in dialogue as they attempt to give expression to their spiritual experience of the world as trustworthy and loving. To give up the "authority" of a creed or set of doctrines is indeed a risk. But it is a risk worth taking.

7

In View of Other Religions

A focal point for criticism of any effort to think theologically in our time is the extent to which it is possible from a given theological position to interact positively with people of other religious traditions. No theology can be considered adequate to the present situation which does not allow for mutual learning and respectful dialogue with people of other faiths.

A dialogically open mind would have been a virtue in any age. But in our time it has become something more like a necessity. Just a generation or so ago, it was possible for most Christians in America and Europe to ignore other religions. Other religions were confronted only in slide presentations of missionaries returning from the "foreign fields" of service, or perhaps in the pages of *National Geographic* magazine. But by the early 1970s, radical changes were afoot. North America and Europe themselves became foreign mission fields, and city streets and airports at times seemed jammed with adherents of numerous religions, each seeking converts. Whereas it might at one time have seemed odd to hear a discussion in which an Asian Baptist and an African Roman Catholic relive vigorously the divisions which took place in sixteenth-century Europe, it now hardly turns your head to find a heated debate going on in a university snack shop in which American or European students heatedly debate divisions which took place in Asia more than a millennium ago!

In the absence of an officially sanctioned religion, America especially has been a place in which hundreds, even thousands, of religions, sects, heresies, divisions and groups are able to flourish.

Europe is increasingly experiencing the same sort of thing. On both continents, immigration from the Near and Far Eastern lands have greatly increased the numbers of inhabitants who adhere to Islam, Hinduism, and Buddhism.

The speed of travel and communications has made us once and for all a global community. Each and every culture is being affected and influenced by other cultures. The resulting pluralism which is present in all areas of life is especially evident in the religious sphere. We now know more about other religions than we ever have before. The holy books of non-Christian religions are easily available in trade paperback versions, and these are obviously selling well.

The full tide of religious pluralism is upon us and it is simply impossible to ignore other religions. Cross-fertilization is happening in any case. The question for theology is whether this radical pluralism will be encountered as a threat to be overcome or as an opportunity to be grasped.

The most conservative forms of Christian theology continue to teach that Christianity is absolute, that it is the one true religion.[1] Evaluations of other religions range from the charitable view that these are "sincere errors" to the more belligerent view that they are demonic deceptions. On the plane of dialogue, the conservatives still insist that Christianity should have the floor.

Especially in America, conservative theology is best known for its "battle" over the Bible, its fortress-like and sometimes auto-cannibalistic defense of biblical authority. The Bible is viewed as the one true revelation of God for all people. The Bible must be seen as infallible, as free from any errors of commission and omission. Therefore, whatever view of other religions we hold, the conservatives insist that view must come directly from the Bible.

It would be very difficult to find from a direct reading of the Bible much ground for openness toward other religions. The Hebrew Bible tells mainly of individual, family and national struggles to repel the syncretistic temptations from the religions of neighbors and conquerors. Critical scholarship informs us that the religious beliefs and practices of the ancient Hebrews were in fact molded by such syncretistic interaction. But this is rarely acknowledged in the biblical text, and conservative theologians tend to be hostile to such conclusions. We do find in the Hebrew

Bible things such as Qoheleth's rather cosmopolitan and world weary conclusions that "all is vanity." But that piece of divine revelation is not long dwelt upon in conservative theology.

In the Christian testament as well, we find the struggles of the early church in first the Jewish and then the Greco-Roman context. Its purpose is proclamation and proselytism. The mother religion, Judaism, is painted as a negative foil in the later writings. Paul's appearance in Athens might be taken as a lesson in dialogue, but again, his clear purpose was proclamation and proselytism.

In short, whatever sanction one finds in the Bible for sympathetic treatment of other religions comes only through reflective inference on ethical ideals found there. For those disinclined toward sympathetic toleration in the first place, these reflective inferences are simply submerged in direct readings of holy wars, prophetic condemnations of syncretism, invectives against "the Jews" and visions of a final Armageddon in which the foes of God are finally exterminated. The Bible has not equipped conservative theology with a sympathetic doctrine of other religions.

If the Bible is viewed as the "one true revelation of God," what can conservatives say of the holy books of other religions? Again, the responses vary. Most charitably this approach must see these holy books as human inventions on the same level as all other books beside the Bible. They can contain good stories, even useful advice, just as many books contain useful advice. But it must always be maintained that the Bible is a qualitatively different book. Less charitable words for the holy books of other religions are also written by conservative theologians.

Quite understandably, the conservative Christians do not find much sympathy for other religions, and the Leitmotif of their view is found generally in the "no other ..." verses such as Exodus 20:3; Deuteronony 6:14; Joshua 24:16; Jeremiah 6:7; Daniel 3:29: 12:32; Acts 4:12; I Corinthians 8:4, etc.

In this theology, there is a rather direct movement from the finality of God's revelation in the Bible, to the absolute uniqueness of Christ, to the conclusion that other religions are false and in no way can lead to salvation. The only aim of the Gospel can be conversion, the hope that people of other faiths will give up that faith and become Christians. Where dialogue and learning from other faiths is encouraged in conservative circles, such as in the statement of the International Congress on World Evangelism, its purpose is clearly and only as a tactic leading to conversion to Christianity.[2] You need to understand the "needs" of people before you can convert them. Sensitive "listening" is therefore a tool for proselytism.

Although certainly more academic in its approach than the conservatives, continental new orthodox theologians found themselves pushed toward many similar positions and statements where other religions are concerned. We can take the views of Karl Barth as paradigmatic.[3] This is also appropriate because of the very great influence the teaching and writing of Barth has had on the more exploratory theologians among the conservatives.

For reasons having to do more or less exclusively with the European context and not as a result of reflection on the meaning of religious pluralism, Karl Barth was struck by the idea of a radicalized christology. To know nothing but Christ and Christ crucified was Barth's answer to confusion of his time. We cannot know God except as God reveals Godself in Jesus Christ. The source for our knowledge of Jesus Christ is the Bible, particularly the Christian New Testament. Once these elements are in place, it matters little that the new orthodoxy preferred to avoid statements about the nature of God's revelation in the Bible and refused to mouth the conservative pet phrases concerning that revelation. The stage is set in any case for an essentially negative reading of other religious faiths.

Barthians stressed the absolute center of God's revelation of Godself in Jesus Christ as mediated through the New Testament. Once one is painted into that corner, there is little room for movement in the encounter with other faiths. God can only be known by self revelation. God is revealed only in Jesus Christ. What then of other faiths?

Barth said that "religion" was mankind's attempts to find God, a God who could only be known by self-revelation. Therefore, religions are no way to salvation, no way to find God. At best they are useless. At worst they actually hinder one from recognizing God's self-revelation and are therefore a form of rebellion and unbelief! It is little wonder that Barthians are not being eagerly pursued as partners in dialogue by people of other faiths.

It would be wrong, however, simply to equate Barthians with the conservatives. For although Barth's radical christology does not hold us in good stead in terms of a sympathetic approach to other religions, it did allow Barth to hear a word of prophetic criticism concerning Christianity which the conservatives miss. For Barth insisted that whatever negative judgments were given about the world's religions, these same judgments applied equally, perhaps even primarily, to the Christian church itself. If one takes that pronouncement seriously, Barth cannot be accused of simple cultural chauvinism. Barth's radical christology was primarily a criticism of the Christian church. Only secondarily was it a criticism of other religions. Nevertheless, it is a theology hardly suited to the present situation as we attempt to make our way peacefully among the labyrinth of religious pluralism.

Moderate ecumenical theology has been unhappy with the arrogant tone of condemnation toward other religions most often found among the conservatives. Ecumenical theology, taking its cues from mission workers who found very much positive in other religious traditions and following the tone set by the World Council of Churches and by the Second Vatican Council, has been exploring positions in which other religious traditions can be viewed in a positive light, allowing for mutual respect between the traditions.

In coming toward a position which reflects our real situation of extreme religious pluralism, this moderate ecumenical theology must be seen as a great stride forward from the conservative position. However, like the conservatives, even the most open and sympathetic approaches toward other religions among the moderates have been undermined by the historic demands of particularity found in Christian theology and christology.

Moderate ecumenical theology usually begins by outlining a rather strong, perhaps exaggerated, distinction between "natural" revelation – that knowledge of God which is open to every human being – and "special" revelation, that knowledge of God which Godself must impart. The more we can know through the channels of natural revelation, the more "knowledge of God" we can legitimately ascribe to the teachings found in other religions. The main thing other religions lack, according to this theology, is the special revelation found in Christianity.

Generally speaking, what we can know through natural revelation, from creation itself, is that God exists, that God is good, that the creation, including human beings, is in need of redemption. Therefore, other religions can be seen as pathways toward Christ, as preparation for the specific Christian revelation concerning the means God has chosen for redemption of the world. Therefore, there is so very much in other religions which can be affirmed! In fact, we can even learn from other religions in areas of general revelation, the knowledge of God which is open to all people. On this level, there can be true mutual appreciation.

But this theology must assume that on the level of specific revelation, on the level of God's plan of salvation for the world, religions other than Christianity will ultimately fall short. Other religious traditions are in need of "fulfillment" by Christian revelation. Other religions are paths leading to the gates of salvation. But Christian revelation is needed to enter the gates.

Although moderate ecumenical theologians were less enthusiastic about drawing conclusions about the damnation of people of other faiths than were their conservative colleagues, their theology did still imply that those outside the Christian religion would be excluded from "salvation," however that be defined. Where salvation is clearly seen as having to do with life after death, the problem centered on how it would be possible for God to damn eternally the majority of humanity who, because of accident of birth, never had the chance to hear the Christian message. And where salvation is viewed in more historical categories, it still made God seem unjust and arbitrary to insist that only Christianity was the route to salvation. Furthermore, it contradicted what we were learning about the complex social organization of non-Christian societies, many of whom exhibited at least as keen a sense of justice as do Christian societies. Moderate theologians began seeking ways out of this impasse their theology had created, trying to find ways in which Christians could affirm that true salvation could be found in other religious traditions.

Probably the best known such attempt was Karl Rahner's idea of the "anonymous Christian."[4] Rahner began by asserting that God wills that all people should find salvation. Through the creation itself God reveals Godself, and therefore all people have received revelation. All revelation leads to salvation. Therefore all religions can be seen as part of God's plan of salvation for humanity. People who follow another religious tradition than Christianity, but who lead exemplary moral lives and truly worship

God from within that religious tradition, may be viewed as "Christians," even if they themselves neither know of Christianity nor accept the label personally. We may view them as "anonymous" Christians.

Rahner's views follow from an expanded christology in which "Christ" is no longer seen as confined to the Christian tradition. Similarly, Hans Küng[5] has asked us to abandon "ecclesiocentrism" in the name of this expanded christology, a christology affected by Karl Barth as well as Catholic sources. Jesus Christ can be seen as the "norm" for all people without assuming that one finds Jesus Christ only among Christians. Other religions are the ordinary way of salvation for humanity, while Christianity represents the extraordinary way for the people of the Christian faith.

But what Rahner and Küng give to other religions on the one hand, they take back on the other. For both of them, there is a time-limitation on the way of salvation through other religions. In one way or another, at one time or another, other religions will cease to be ways of salvation and be displaced by Christianity, or at least by explicit recognition that the Christian God is God of everyone. Rahner seems to say that the time comes when a person first hears the Christian gospel. Küng, more attentive to the social channels through which a religious message travels, says that it will happen only when Christianity has become enough of the part of a culture for a person to be presented with an authentic choice between the Christian message and that of the other religion. In either case, however, the time is limited. The ideology of Christian particularism finally displaces the reality of pluralism in moderate ecumenical theology.

A theologian who has moved beyond the moderate ecumenical position is John Hick.[6] John Hick uses an analogy from astronomy and speaks of a "Copernican revolution" in theology which comes about in response to the modern situation of pluralism. In Hick's analogy, moderate ecumenical theology remains confined to a "Ptolemaic" universe. While the challenge of new questions can be met in this theology by adding cosmic circles which enlarge the scope of the system, the system itself remains bound to a center, which is anathema to pluralism. Christological particularism, the myth that God was uniquely incarnate in Jesus Christ, is this center. So long as theology clings to this central doctrine, it can never truly accept and move comfortably within the pluralistic matrix of thought.

In contrast, John Hick proposes a theocentric rather than christocentric theology. The true object of all religious devotion, God as Godself, or, in Hick's preferred terms, the "Eternal One," is not and cannot be known and articulated directly, but always and only through mediation of religions. No religion can give more than a partial picture of the Eternal One. Therefore, for example, it would be possible to affirm that Jesus Christ is an absolutely true revelation of God without having to insist on the opposite, that all other revelations of God in other religions are necessarily false or even inferior. Knowledge of God in other religions may broaden the Christian understanding of God without competing with it or attempting to displace it.

In his historical reconstruction, Hick makes much of Karl Jaspers' "axial period," roughly 800 to 200 BCE.[7] It was during this period of time that, in China, India, the Middle East and the Mediterranean worlds, the major religious traditions of human-kind crystalized out of their tribalistic and animistic origins. It was a period when the Eternal One "pressed in" on humanity, and new spiritual insights were gained in cultures unconnected with one another in any direct sense. The spiritual insights which took strong root in one culture may differ from those which took strong root in another. Therefore, one religious tradition may emphasize the "personal" nature of God and hold the impersonal qualities of God as an undercurrent. Another culture may emphasize the impersonal nature of God and hold the personal qualities as an undercurrent. Such surface contradictions are important, but not final. For Hick feels that especially in the practical area of worship, it is possible to see that people are responding, within a tradition which mediates language, methods and so forth, to the same Eternal One. God has many names.

From Hick's perspective, one may wholly affirm the truth and integrity of all religious traditions. One may enter into true dialogue with those of other faiths without any hidden agenda of "conversion." One may view the teachings of other religious traditions as opportunities to expand the horizons of one's own understanding. People of all religions can be seen as one family, united by the theocentrism of each tradition.

Of the theological options discussed above, Hick's theocentric position has taken the situation of pluralism most to heart and has most about it to commend in terms of working beyond an implied hierarchy of religions.

A postliberal perspective on other religions can best be articulated in conversation with the theocentrism of John Hick. Hick's theology has by far the most well developed and sensitive understanding of other religions. I will therefore outline my views in the form of a series of questions directed at Hick's theology.

Granting that all articulated doctrines of God are partial and in that sense relative, Hick takes as axiomatic the assertion that each is a partial description of an actually existing and external "transcendent reality." No one doctrine of God may be taken as absolute or exhaustive, yet he insists on a "basic religious conviction ... that the realm of religious experience and belief is our human response to a transcendent divine reality."[8] Therefore, this transcendent divine reality must be external to us. This is very important for Hick because "... It is the conviction, in other words, that religion is not, as a totality, illusion and self-deception."[9]

Hick employs, among other devices, Paul Tillich's "God above the God of theism,"[10] as well as Gordon Kaufman's distinction between the "real God and the available God,"[11] to make this point of difference. Without this distinction, we have no assurance that religion as a totality is not illusion and self-deception.

Is this way of setting the choice before us really intelligible? It may well be justified to hold as a personal conviction that the "real God" exists. But we cannot forget that those who have spoken of this distinction between God and God in modern theology have been forced to the conclusion that this "real God" must remain an "utterly unknowable X." We might as well quit speaking about it. Yet Hick's theocentrism takes as its basic conviction, as that which assures us that religion as a totality is not illusion and self-deception, an attribute (existence) of an utterly unknowable X.

By defining the choice before us in this manner, that either religion is a response to an external divine transcendence or it is illusion and self-deception, Hick raises the stakes too high for what is essentially a paradoxical assertion on a theological level. We are all welcome to our personal convictions concerning the attributes of an utterly unknowable X. But these personal convictions are not a good starting point for the public statements of theology.

Postliberalism, if it is to succeed, must be able to show that we can dispense with statements about an utterly unknowable X and still not be forced to conclude that religion in its totality is illusion and self-deception.

The problem this basic conviction of Hick's creates for theology is further illustrated by his preferred terms for God *an sich*. He has a special affection for the "Eternal One." He likes this term because it unites both personal and nonpersonal traditions in theology. But again, there is a great distance between an utterly unknowable X and the Eternal One. Already Hick has now ascribed existence, eternality and oneness to an utterly unknowable X. His God *an sich* begins to resemble the "available God, which is essentially a mental or imaginative construct" after all.

There is a logical and inescapable progression here which needs elucidation. Once we have ascribed any attribute at all to this God *an sich*, once we violate the axiom that God *an sich* is anything other than an utterly unknowable X, it is both logical and inescapable that this God *an sich* will become more interesting and worthy of theological attention than any or even all of our partial and halting confessional constructions of God. Very soon we are speculating freely about God *an sich*, whose attributes are existence, eternality, oneness, and . . . .

The more we think about, speculate on and speak of this God, the more this God becomes yet one more of our mental constructs, one more among the many. How many examples are there in which a religion, philosophy or social movement began as an attempt to transcend and "unite" all others – only to end up as yet one more among the many? While affirming religious pluralism, an approach to other religious traditions which ends only in creating yet one more "truer-than-the-others" theology is not a desired outcome. By taking what is appropriate as a personal conviction and then elevating that to a basic conviction for public theology, Hick's theocentrism commits a category error which will inevitably lead in the direction of establishing yet one more "truer-than-the-others" religion.

As I see it, our only way out of this dilemma is to begin a public theology with the firm conviction that God *an sich* is an utterly unknowable X and that what we cannot speak about, of that we must remain silent! Theology is richer and not poorer for this silence. For then we are unburdened to seek truth about the plurality of religions in the full face of the many Gods of humankind.

Again, another problem with Hick's starting point for theology is that although this conviction, that all religions are pointing toward the same external transcendent reality, may facilitate a unity or "family" feeling among religious believers, it neglects the fact that an increasingly large area of our pluralistic world is inhabited by people who are explicitly atheist. Must all those people who cannot give assent to the basic conviction that God *an sich* exists be *ipso facto* excluded from our family? This seems to be a necessary conclusion of Hick's theocentrism. Perhaps it is not his intention, but I am not aware of his addressing this question directly and must infer this conclusion from what he has written. If our religious experiences are partial but true responses to an actually existing, external transcendent reality, then we can only conclude that atheists are at best inadequate in their experiences, or at worst stubbornly wrong-headed. In any case, they are not "one of us." I do not see how Hick can avoid this conclusion, unless he resorts to something analogous to Rahner's teaching about the "anonymous Christian" in order to sneak the atheist under our family umbrella after all. Having forged ahead with a Copernican revolution in theology, it would be sad to find that we must return to Ptolemaic expansion of cosmic circles once again.

This problem is also solved when we simply refuse to entertain in public theology any statements about an utterly unknowable X. We will then treat atheism as a legitimate mental construction of God and proceed to evaluate it according to the same standards as any other theological construction. We will need to inquire of the professing atheist what he or she means by a construction of God which negates the existence of God. In other words, we will need to ask for a description of the God being negated in order to understand what the person is truly trying to express by his or her atheism. (Chances are, we may not believe in *that* God either . . . !)

Can an atheist negate not just particular constructions of God, but rather God *an sich*? Is it possible to assert that the utterly unknowable X does not exist? Yes, it is possible to hold this as a personal conviction. But as a public doctrine it is as inadequate as the theist's personal convictions about the utterly unknowable X.

Both are claims to know something about something which is defined as utterly unknowable. Neither claim, therefore, has any place in a public theology.

When either the theist or the atheist brings personal convictions about something utterly unknowable into the public forum of life, all we can do is ask for more information about the consequences of these convictions. In the postliberal perspective, all utterly unknowable Xs are equal, beyond good and evil, beyond existence and nonexistence. All utterly unknowable Xs simply do not make any difference. The only transcendent reality that can make a difference to us is the transcendent reality of the human soul and spirit, an internal transcendence, not an external transcendence. The only God that can make a difference is a God within history. God enters into history as we mentally construct God's image and attempt to articulate what God is for us. An "available God" is the only God we have.

All utterly unknowable Xs are equal. Are then all articulated Gods equal? Again, this question is made more elusive than it need be if we take Hick's personal convictions about God *an sich* as our starting point. According to Hick's explanation, all experiences of God are partial, and all attempts to formulate doctrines of God must also be partial. Like the blind men describing an elephant, each giving a true but partial description, depending on which part of the elephant they are touching, our descriptions of God in theology and in daily life are partial. Even seemingly contradictory statements (God is personal/God is impersonal) are unified on the higher level of God *an sich*. Just as the man holding the trunk of the elephant insists that elephants are soft and round, while the man pressing on the side of the elephant insists that elephants are firm and flat, these contradictory assertions are unified on the higher level of the elephant itself, which includes both realities. So we are genuinely left wondering whether all partial descriptions of God are true. If not, how do we sort through them? Could one blind man actually be touching a tiger rather than an elephant?

Hick obviously prefers the "historical" pictures of God which originated in the axial period and form the foundations for the world's great religions. The tribal and animistic religious views which preceded this lack majesty and university. Hick strongly implies that humanity took a great step forward during this period, and we may infer, therefore, that those understandings which preceded this period are seen as inferior. Developments after this period, as found for example in Jesus and Mohammed, are seen as extensions of what was crystalized during this axial period, rather than as anything qualitatively new. Perhaps it would be possible to formulate an image of God which has nothing to do with those images which crystalized during the axial period, but it is hard to imagine that such an image would carry conviction. Therefore, we must conclude that while Hick sees all constructions of God as partial, some are more partial than others. But he is very unclear as to the guidelines for sorting out more adequate from less adequate constructions.

Postliberal theology assumes that God *an sich* is an utterly unknowable X. Therefore, while we agree that all of our articulated views of God are partial, we do not seek to find anything "behind" or "beyond" these partial images which they describe. It makes no sense to insist that these are partial descriptions of an utterly unknowable X, for again, we would be then claiming to know something about something which is defined as unknowable. It is a misunderstanding of what is meant by defining something as utterly unknowable.

Only articulated constructions of God can concern postliberal theology. This is not to say that our religious experiences are illusion and self-deception. The religious experiences of human beings are so real and so resistant to reductionist criticism that we find the number of people claiming such experiences growing even in scientifically advanced societies, both capitalist and socialist. That religious experiences are real and not illusion is simply an evident fact. Like the existence of a mountain, it is just there. There is no need to "defend" the reality of human religious experience. We should rather reflect on its meaning.

In reflecting on human religious experience, we see immediately that such experiences are extremely diverse, are largely affected by cultural conditioning, and are articulated in many different ways. Even within one culture there may be no exact agreement among people as to what does or does not constitute a religious experience. Our reflections, which take such facts into consideration, may lead us to conclusions quite different from any one particular first-level articulation by a person who has had a religious experience. But that does not lead us to conclude that what that person has experienced is simply "self-deception." Why should it?

But insisting on the existence of an utterly unknowable X is irrelevent to this issue of whether religion as a totality is real or illusion, or self-deception. An utterly unknowable X can neither preserve the integrity of religion nor undermine it. It can simply be dispensed with. Then theology can move forward to concern itself with the plurality of mental constructions of God. Rather than constantly seeking to look "behind" these images to some utterly unknowable X, postliberal theology would rather see these images as reflectors, and ask questions concerning the ones who formulate these many images. Theology in postliberal perspective indeed studies the human constructions of God. It attempts to construct ever more adequate and useful constructions of God. It does so for humans' sake.

I agree with Hick that God has many names. But I also agree with the conservatives that there are true and false images of God. The view of God a person holds has rather direct political and public consequences. It sets the parameters of action. It both establishes and reflects a particular value system. Postliberal theology insists that there are both true and false Gods. We must establish the true Gods and maintain atheism in the face of the false Gods. Our knowledge of which Gods are true and which are false is based on an ethical evaluation of the consequences of belief in each.

Before we get into the principles of such evaluation, I would like to point out one more significant point of difference between John Hick's theology and my own. It is a question of "place."

Hick is much more inclined than I am to think of religious dialogue taking place on a large scale. I think it is wonderful when large religious bodies or academic institutions sponsor study groups and provide platforms for religious dialogue between learned and clerical representatives of differing religious traditions. At least, it gives scholars something useful to work on. At best (as has been the case in Hick's own Birmingham), when people of different faiths see their leaders interacting in a respectful and friendly manner, it may help to build bridges of trust between urban neighborhoods where only suspicion and hatred were found before.

My views, however, have been worked out in a different

context, a context in which close interaction with people of other religious traditions took place on a face-to-face basis. My most significant experiences were teaching a number of times a course on world religions in an international setting where all of the world's major faith traditions were represented among the students; and close and active participation over a six-year period in a small Friends Meeting in Vienna, Austria, in which all of the major faiths were represented. These were not "Christian converts," but rather people of various faith backgrounds who came together to worship in the silent Quaker style. My views reflect this context.

I do not think my views are "anti"-institutional. But I am much less inclined than are some writers on interreligious dialogue to think immediately of the institutional implications of my views. My views reflect my own struggle to understand things on a face-to-face level of interaction. I will be most happy if the views I express here are found useful and built upon, revised and supplemented, by people coming to these issues from other background experiences, including that of work within institutions.

What is the goal and purpose of religion? In answering this question, we need to keep certain things in mind. We need to be respectful of the answers which emerge from within the many religious traditions themselves. We also want to avoid as much as possible any explicit or implicit judgmental ranking of religious traditions. Even by identifying an "essence" of religion, we run the risk of an implied ranking of the traditions according to how each measures up to this essence. We must identify a goal and purpose of religion which applies equally to any religious tradition, including atheism, without implicitly singling one or a few of them out as "better" than others.

We also want to avoid the nebulous conclusion that all religious expressions are equally good or equally bad, equally useful or equally useless. If religions are all one thing or another, our conclusions simply cannot be very interesting. Some criteria must apply in sorting through the multitude of religious responses of humankind. Postliberal theology seeks that criteria in the sphere of ethics. Therefore, from a postliberal perspective, the question of the goal and purpose of religion must be posed from a strictly pragmatic point of view.

My answer is this. The goal and purpose of things religious is:

1. to allow each human being to feel recognized and confirmed as significant and as having personal meaning;

2. to nurture in each human being those virtues of spiritual substance which are manifest in attitudes of tolerance, respect, critical self-esteem, love for others, generosity, concern for justice, a sense of being a world citizen, and a sense of responsibility and desire to live peacefully with all species within the earth's ecosphere;

3. to facilitate the creation of social arrangements which foster a vital environment of purpose and values based on social connectedness of this kind.

It is assumed that these are three aspects of one continuous movement toward social maturity. In our situation of global crises, in which holocausts of war, of genocide and of ecological collapse stare us menacingly in the face, it represents a movement toward species survival as well. This continuous movement is shared as a goal by the entire discipline of humanistic studies, as well as by the best understandings of what we would like to accomplish through scientific research and learning. Many of the problems we are having in our educational system, it seems to me, stem directly from allowing petty dictators and self-seekers to rise to positions of resposibility in our educational system who have long since placed self and/or departmental advancement ahead of this overarching goal of learning.

As we enter into religious dialogue from a postliberal perspective, it is this movement toward social maturity which has to be kept on the mental horizon. Those religious expressions which foster movement in the direction indicated here are to be encouraged. Those which tend to move against this current are to be seen as stagnant and to be questioned and discouraged. A few points are in need of clarification.

First, there is no one view of God which is the "right" view, and by which all others can be measured or ranked. Any construction of God which helps people in their movement along this continuum is true. Any view which causes stagnation is false.

Secondly, since what we seek is movement along a continuum, we must expect that even one individual's view of God will change sometimes quite dramatically, over time. We may take here as a metaphor those theories of moral development which speak of developmental "stages."[12] We would not expect, for example, a six-year-old to give the same answers to questions of right and wrong as would a teenager. We expect these two to be in different stages of development. An eighteen-year-old who answers as a six-year-old would be seen as having stagnated. Likewise if a six-year-old answered as an eighteen-year-old, we would have reason to doubt if the child really understood what he or she were saying. Therefore, though the two would disagree as to the specifics of what is right or wrong in a given set of circumstances, we can affirm both of them in the truth of their moral reasoning and judgments without lapsing into a nihilistic relativism. Nor does this need to imply a hierarchical ranking of the stages of development.

Similarly, we may affirm as true a view of God, let us say, as "the one watching you all the time and who punishes you when you do wrong," if such a view were coming from a child at that stage of moral development in which the child is learning to internalize basic rules of social behavior. Such a God might be a meaningful aid in this process of internalization. By acting as a sort of omniscient externalized and reified conscience, such a God might be helping the child along our continuum, but the same view coming from an otherwise mentally developed adult, much less from a preacher or theologian, would be a clear sign of stagnation.

Thirdly, and closely related to what has just been said, a view of God which is needed and necessary at one stage of a person's life for dramatic behavioral change cannot be universalized. The best example I can think of is that of talking with people who have been substance abusers or have been hardened criminals in prison. The testimony of such people generally points toward constructions of God quite different from one operative in my life. It is also clear that the construction of God operative in my life would not have had the "power" to turn such people around on their paths of destruction. Is this not proof even on my own terms, I asked myself, that their construction of God is somehow more true than my own?

I have come to see that I can affirm the view of God in the preaching of a skid row missionary or a prison minister without assuming that the view must be true for everyone at all times. Our only criteria can be whether this particular construction of God, in the time and place it appears, is helping people along the continuum. Similarly, I have met many people who have had rather dramatic religious experiences and some years later, feel they have lost something of that experience. "God used to be so close to me! I prayed and talked to God all the time. Now I just don't feel that way anymore. What went wrong?"

My answer is that their construction of God has changed from the time of that intense religious experience. But that does not mean they have "lost" anything at all. The question to be examined, rather, is whether the construction of God they now hold is helping them in their current circumstances along this ethical continuum.

Again, since what we seek is growth and movement in our constructions of God, we need not assume that all humans must move at the same speed. We need not assume that all humans will eventually reach the same understandings. Even though we speak of growth and movement and use ethical criteria for judging this, we are not assuming an evolutionary or any other kind of hierarchy in constructions of God. An astrophysicist may well have a very different view of the universe from mine. But my very rudimentary understanding of the universe does not necessarily mean stagnation according to our criteria. If my goal were to become an astrophysicist, and I had learned nothing more about quarks and black holes in my thirty-six years than I have, then that would surely mean stagnation.

Likewise, specialists in theology need not assume that everyone must come to see things in exactly the same way as does the theologian. Just as the astrophysicist will have a different understanding of the universe from mine, so the theologian may have a rather different view of God from the nonspecialist. But this need not imply in either case any kind of elitism or hierarchy of views. It is rather an embrace of pluralism.

As theologians, we must keep our ethical criteria always on the mental horizon. This will help us use insight, sensitivity and wisdom in employing the iconoclastic function of theology. We want to use it to build up the web of purposeful connections rather than simply to destroy those tentative threads of meaning which people have created in their lives.

Finally, from what has been said, it is by now clear that a postliberal approach to other religious traditions seeks neither conversion from one religion to another nor a "ranking" of the religions according to some external value system, nor in "unification" of the religious traditions on some higher, transcendental level.[13] Postliberalism rather seeks to encourage people toward growth along this ethical continuum from *within* each of the religious traditions.

Although postliberalism will not set up prescriptive ethical norms over which hairs may then be split, the general direction to be encouraged is clear. And sources of strength and encouragement for moving along this continuum can be found among all religions, whether Buddhist, Baptist, Bahai or Bhakti; whether Anglican, African Traditional, Albigensian or Atheist.

8

Instead of a Conclusion

On a visit to Harvard University I had the privilege of hearing the theologian Harvey Cox address an audience on the current popularity of "religion" in American society. Harvey Cox, of course, is best known for his best-selling book *The Secular City*, which in the mid-1960s extolled the secularization of American society. At that time Cox was predicting that traditional religious thought would be eclipsed by a kind of sophisticated and cosmopolitan pluralism, and argued that this was in keeping with the perspective the Judeo-Christian tradition had given us on the place of human beings in society and in the world.

The popularity of Cox's book, quite unusual for a treatise of academic theology, can perhaps best be explained by the fact that Cox had gathered together and popularized certain assumptions about the future of religion which have been with us at least since the eighteenth century. Needless to say, for these people, the strong resurgence of fundamentalist Christianity and Judaism, as well as the appearance of fakirs and gurus of every stripe, right in the middle of the secular city, came as a bit of a surprise. In his lecture that day, Cox rightly noted that just as secularity is not all bad, the current resurgence of interest in religion is not all good.

The fact of the matter is that the ebb and flow of interest in religion has been an American characteristic since its beginning. If we are indeed experiencing the course of the "Fourth Great Awakening," one observation is unavoidable. With each such Awakening, the religious commitment resulting has been less enduring, more superficial and more dependent on the media (rather than the message) to sustain any sense of a movement at all.

Although sociologists of various schools have tried to use "scientific data" to map out for us the future of religion in our society, the results are contradictory and inconclusive. Finally, the religious thinker must make his or her own assumptions about the future of religious thought, and this will have a profound effect on that person's thinking about God. Although my own assumptions can muster only partial support from the "experts," I do think that the present surge of interest in "traditional" religious ideas is but a passing episode within the larger picture of the decline of such religion. This decline has not been and will not be unilinear. But the general direction of decline, which began as far back as the sixteenth century, is to my mind quite clear.

This does not mean that religious thinking will disappear. It means, rather, that religion as a system of external control will continue to decrease in significance. People will increasingly claim their right to make their own decisions in matters of faith and practice. The political power of the church as an institution, its ability to dictate public policy, has been broken, and I do not expect its return.[1] Whatever power the church as an institution has to dictate policy is now limited exclusively to its own membership. And even there, I think that the American Roman Catholic experience is paradigmatic for the future. That is, decisions of faith and practice will become increasingly localized and carried out "under the heads" of the institutional hierarchy.

This is not to say that religion will become strictly a "private" affair. Particularly in matters of service to humanity, congregational and communal decision-making and execution of programs will become even more the norm. The moral authority of the church and its leaders will continue to affect the public arena. But again it bears repeating, the political power of the church as an institution, its ability to dictate public policy, is ended. As this fact is grasped with increasing clarity, it will have a profound effect on the construction of God in the religious thought of believers. Already one is more likely to hear of God spoken of in many churches in terms of a friend, a companion, even a "fellow sufferer who understands," than as the all-powerful and commanding God of traditional Christianity.

I therefore place myself among those thinkers popularized by Harvey Cox who assume that demystification and not re-mystification is the path on which we travel, for better or for worse. But having said that, we would do well to remind ourselves of the observation of Ernst Bloch, that "the real metaphysical questions are more enduring than the mythological, transcendental answers" which have been given to them.[2] Indeed, it is the contemplation of these questions which, in the modern world, stands between us as humans and us as little cogs in a machine beyond our ability either to understand or direct. We can recover the "mystery" of our life in the cosmos without a remystification of nature in the older sense. What is at stake is our attitude toward the natural world, of which we are a part. One need not cower in fear of an animistically conceived natural order to experience the mystery of the necessary dependence we as human beings have in relation to the natural order. One need not fear the "ocean spirit" to recognize that we cannot pollute our waters indefinitely.

The all-powerful and commanding God of the church as a political institution able to dictate public policy is going and gone. We are forced by circumstances, therefore, to construct new images of God which will answer the needs of human community in the present situation. But because the question of God arises in the first place in answer to the problematic character of human nature, it is by no means certain that this all-powerful and commanding God will not simply be replaced by an all-powerful and commanding state. If we exchange servitude to God for servitude to the state, what have we gained?

The time has come, as the late Michael Harrington observed, for religious humanists and secular humanists finally to end their conflict. Both, says Harrington, "should be appalled by the *de facto* atheism in late capitalist society ... It is thoughtless, normless, selfish, hedonistic individualism."[3] And this is no less true of what is preached by our "television evangelists" than of purveyors of a playboy philosophy. A society which chokes in its own pollution resulting from the production of its wealth, which allows the "free market" to set policy even while millions of its people are put homeless on the streets, which spends billions on military programs while education flounders and lack of affordable medical care and even actual malutrition remain central concerns for large segments of its population, is *de facto* atheistic, regardless of the pious-sounding pronouncements of its rulers.

We can no longer insist that a morality which would stand against this *de facto* atheism is grounded in the transcendental commandments of an all-powerful God. Yet the voices of the biblical prophets, as well as countless others in our tradition who have called us to love and justice in our public life, are part of our heritage. The challenge we face now is to draw on these riches of our heritage to create a political morality to which the wide variety of believers and non-believers can give assent and commitment.

Throughout the reflections in this book I have tried to stay as close as possible to a line of inquiry which might be broadly characterized as phenomenological. We began by looking at the human condition, which I characterized as "split" between a transcendent and godlike mental capacity and a weak and mortal physical body. Faced with this dilemma of being, humans devise various strategies for denying the predicament. We create, in short, through the use of symbols, all kinds of immortality projects behind which to hide. Although these immortality projects demand innumerable sacrifices of us, life would simply be intolerable without the shield against reality which they provide. The anxiety produced by the human consciousness of death is more than a creature can take undiluted. Only a god could bear it. Yet every time we humans try to play god, even in small and limited spheres, much less on the grand scale of the modern nation state, the result is always negative and oppressive. It now threatens our entire race with extinction.

For centuries, we could at least rely on God to save us. We could throw our anxiety on God and ask for divine intervention. Now we find even that refuge of last resort is closed off. We have killed God by our own analysis. Is it any wonder that Nietzsche chose to announce this through the mouth of a madman?

The pride and glee which once accompanied the phrase "humankind come of age" has definitely faded. We are indeed on our own. But now we see what miserable creatures we really are. Our sense of pride and power is based on lies of our own creation which now threaten to consume us. To paraphrase a once popular song, we are "a walking contradiction, partly truth, but mostly fiction."

I truly wish that as a conclusion to this book I could outline a clear and concise three-point plan for answering the human problem, preferably one that could be poetically alliterated and easily adapted to high-priced weekend seminars at scenic mountain retreats. But it can't be done. That would simply add to the many fictions which already flow from the pens of beaming writers hawking their prescriptive solutions.

There is simply no way, short of fiction, to escape what Unamuno called the tragic sense of life.[4] There may be no final solutions, but always and only partial and stumbling answers. I am sure of one thing. It would be a grave mistake to make of "saving humanity" a new immortality project, a new altar on which to sacrifice ourselves and others with us. There is enough of that going around already. Incongruous as it might sound, we somehow have to hold even the goal of saving humanity from extinction in detachment, as a means to another end, and not as an end in itself. But how then can we remain "dead serious" about the project? I don't know.

No, I cannot offer any final solutions. But if we do have a creative, transcending and loving soul and spirit in each of us, then we can affirm that this material life is not all there is to us. That soul and spirit, so far as I can see, do represent a vital force, drawing us toward an amplification of being. If for those following the path of denial this drive for "more life" is perverted into destructiveness, that observation in itself is a criticism of our tendency to view myopically what an amplified life is. It is not a negative reflection on the work of the soul and spirit *per se*.

Therefore, whatever survival strategies we may devise, they will have to begin with a deep and critical probing of the human soul and spirit. This will have to be accompanied by serious and iconoclastic examination of those projects of immortality which our society and culture thrust upon us.

It is a very hard time in which to be optimistic. Projections such as those of the "Club of Rome" do not give us much grounds for optimism. Our cities are full of drug wars and drug-related crime. Violence literally drips before us for everyday consumption. The category of future, taken in isolation, cannot but aggrevate the sense of anxiety under which we already limp. But our religious geniuses – the Buddha, Jesus, and Baal Shem Tov, perhaps some of the Roman Stoics – have given us a vision of life, God's

Kingdom of freedom, in which the future is creatively joined with the present. In this state of living, it seems most possible maximally to internalize the reality of mortality (or in Tillich's terms, Being incorporating Nonbeing)[5] and yet not turn the anxiety thereby produced neurotically and oppressively on others.

The problem with this "solution," of course, is that we human beings don't really want that kind of answer. It is the last thing we want to hear. It is too anticultural, too anarchical; it is too, well, foolish. If we make all of life a "feast of fools," who will plant next year's crops? Perhaps crop-planting also could be made into a game, a party?[6] I am not optimistic about that prospect. Yet I don't think we can abandon it entirely. After all, even Unamuno ended his torturously penetrating book with a chapter on Don Quixote.[7] We are all playing games anyway, trying so hard through our efforts and work to create illusions of meaning and purpose. Why do our games then have to be one big demolition derby?

Humor, not taking life too seriously, laughing even at our most cherished projects, is one tool in our box to keep ourselves humble, yet forward-moving. A sense of life as play is another.[8]

"Playing at the game of life" is a phrase which expresses that vision of living in joy which does not take life too seriously. The basic contradictions of our being cannot be resolved. But is it not possible to live in such a way that recognition of absurdity produces a smile on our face rather than panic in our breast? For that creature who spends most of its life knowing that it will die, experiencing that death in a thousand nightmares, making of the time we do have a humorous and playful sacrifice to whatever lies beyond is the highest form of heroism. This is not the same as denying or ignoring the tragedy of our existence. It is no escape from doing justice. Those figures in our history – the Buddha, Jesus, the Baal Shem Tov among others – who have come the closest to this way of living, all knew only too well the tragic sense of life. Each in his or her own way responded positively to injustice and oppression. But each also had a keen sense of the extreme limitations of the individual. This manifested itself not only in a loving, accepting and forgiving attitude toward the shortcomings of others, but also toward their own shortcomings. These people continue to be our ideal types, the kind of people held up to others as examples to follow.

Although it leaves me open to the criticism of returning to the posture of optimism, I do continue to place a strong hope in the possibility of religious conversion. Our society encourages us to think in terms of dualism. This dualism is reflected in my own religious imaginings. There are Gods of peace and freedom and Gods of war and bondage. Yet I do want to make clear that I see this dualistic presentation of theology as a heuristical and not a metaphysical dualism. The task of theology is to enourage people to move from the worship of Gods of bondage and war toward the worship of Gods of love and freedom. That this task is not impossible is the extent of my optimism.

There are human experiences so deep, so "gut-level," that they demand an increasingly wider context within which to express themselves and to find fulfillment. In such experiences there is a fusion of the whole person such that the restrictions of dualism are dissolved. Our "character armor" (Ernest Becker) is shed in such experiences. If this fusion is discovered in one area of our lives, it will progressively work, if we allow it, to break down barriers in other areas as well.

The German word for experience, *Erfahrung*, points in this direction. *Erfahrung* derives from the verb *erfahren*, which means to learn. This in turn derives from *fahren*, which means to drive or to travel. To experience, therefore, is to engage in movement. Like the ripple of a stone cast into water, these deep human experiences, common to all people, demand a progressively wider context in which to express themselves and find fulfillment. If this movement toward ever wider contexts of expression is constricted, the quality of the original experience will eventually be effected and destroyed.

The experience of God as love is such an experience. In Christian theology it is the absolute center, the power source, of all such experiences. When God is experienced as love, the person is pushed toward ever-widening areas of life in which to express that experience. If this is restricted, the ripples on the water of experience create chaotic patterns. One cannot love God and continue indefinitely to hate others (1 John 4:20f.). Like a rose plucked from the bush, the original experience of God as love will wilt and die if it is restricted from seeking ever-wider contexts within which to express itself and find fulfillment.

Christian theology begins with the experience of God as love.

But there are many other beginning points for human experience which also express this deep, gut-level claim on human relationships. Truly loving lovers experience this wholeness, this dissolving of dualism. It is no accident that religious poets and writers have used the metaphor of lovers to ground their expressions of God as love. The experience of suffering injustice and standing in solidarity with those who suffer injustice is for many people in the modern world such a deep and fusing experience.

Such deep and fusing experiences are available to and happen to all human beings. But we fear the "unprotectedness" of letting go, of walking unfamiliar paths, of allowing these experiences to seek ever wider contexts within which to find expression and fulfillment. It is a human tendency to restrict these experiences and attempt to confine them only to those areas which are familiar. But this attempt to "control" such experiences must finally create chaotic patterns in our lives.

A man may love his wife and hate his neighbor. But if he continues to hate his neighbor, it will ultimately impair the love he has for his wife. His hatred will disfigure his love, and his love will only become whole again as his hatred is diminished. A personal experience of solidarity with those who suffer injustice may not lead today or tomorrow into a universal love for others. But if the flow towards this universal love, which is the natural fruit of such experience, is restricted, the original experience of solidarity will become disformed, disfigured, and will finally be nothing but yet one more kind of hatred.

Our deep, gut-level, fusing experiences are perhaps what seventeenth century English radicals referred to as the "inner light." These English radicals knew that some spark of the inner light could be found in all human beings. To "find that light and speak to it" meant that even though deep, fusing experiences were hidden under layer upon layer of restriction, these experiences are present and can be reached. In postliberal perspective, the goal of theology and religious reflection is to help lift the restrictions people have placed on their experiences and to help people allow once again for their own experiences of fusion to seek ever widening contexts for expression and fulfillment. The goal of theology and religious reflection in postliberal perspective is to break down barriers of dualism which restrict the fusing experiences of the human soul and spirit, bringing each person into that realm of life in which there is no male or female, Jew or Gentile, slave or freeman (Galatians 3) but where people are free from the bondage and fear which create these divisions in the first place.

This can happen. People can find freedom, in peaceful and loving manner, to acknowledge the limitations of being human together, even those limitations whose ultimate form is death. It is the freedom to give over our immortality projects to each other and still stand as whole and independent people, buoyed by the strength of one another.

It is probably not possible to live totally outside the system of construction of immortality projects. To do so would be to live outside human history itself. We have to build our sense of meaning and purpose, necessary for forward movement, on something. And at least as far as we can tell, there are no empirical external sources of meaning and purpose from which to draw. The natural order gives us sunshine and rain and, so long as we don't abuse it, a basically inhabitable and friendly environment within which to live. But in answer to our quest for meaning and purpose in our lives, the cosmos is silent. We have to construct our own visions of meaning and purpose.

It is here that we must finally return to the problem of God. Integral to the construction of meaning and purpose is the construction of an image of God, an image which stands ahead of us, calling us to acts of justice and reconciliation, a God who meets us in those times of quiet meditation when we are most centered on the creative, transcending and loving promptings of the soul and spirit. If we must construct meaning and purpose in our lives, it only makes sense to seek those guiding notions which are the highest. Such symbols have political consequences, eliciting and setting the parameters for human responses in particular situations. And that is the level on which our choice of symbols, of guiding notions, must be made.

For Christians, the God we meet in such moments will likely bear the face of Jesus. For others, this God will have a different face or no face at all. There may be no universals, no collective unconscious, and we certainly have no empirical proof that there is. But we cannot give up the search for meaning. If we are to find it, I am convinced that there, in the deepest level of our being, is the only place left we have to look.

NOTES

Introduction: Approaching the Subject

1. The most accessible short exposition of the deconstructionist approach is Gary Peller, "Reason and the Mob: The Politics of Representation," *TIKKUN*, Vol. II, No. 3 (July/August 1987), pp. 28ff. Unavoidable is Richard Rorty, *Philosophy and the Mirror of Nature* (Princeton: Princeton University Press, 1979). A very interesting exchange on the politics of representation as it relates to "Creationism" and evolution can be found in the Nov./Dec. 1987 issue of *TIKKUN*. As it relates directly to theology, cf. Carl A. Raschke, *The Alchemy of the Word: Language and the End of Theology*, AAR Studies in Religion 20 (Missoula: Scholars Press, 1979); Robert P. Scharlemann, *The Being of God: Theology and the Experience of Truth* (New York: Seabury Press, 1981); Charles Winquist, Mark C. Taylor, Carl A. Raschke, "Theology and the Moment of Deconstruction," part III of C. Raschke, ed., *New Dimensions in Philosophical Theology*, JAAR Thematic Studies XLIX/1 (1982), pp. 71–126; Mark C. Taylor, *Deconstructing Theology* (New York: Crossroad Publishing Company, 1982); also *Erring: A Postmodern A/theology* (Chicago: University of Chicago Press, 1984). A symposium on this book appeared in JAAR LIV/3 (1986), pp. 523–57. Further, Thomas J. J. Altizer, et al., *Deconstruction and Theology* (New York: Crossroad Publishing Company 1982); and most recently, Charles E. Winquist, *Epiphanies of Darkness: Deconstruction in Theology* (Philadelphia: Fortress Press, 1986). Unfortunately, these latter books and articles lack the clarity of style characteristic of Peller and Rorty. Concerning the politics of representation, I share the conclusions of the deconstructionist school. However, I am rather repelled by their deliberately obscure writing style (although I like the word-plays) and their flirtations with theological nihilism. I think it is possible to recognize, as modern theologians have done implicitly for over a century, the death of transcendent subject in theology and still strive for sense and clarity in theological writing and theological thinking. My approach here has been greatly influenced by the more recent essays of Prof. Gordon D. Kaufman. Also, Jens Glebe-Moeller, *A Political Dogmatic* (Philadelphia: Fortress Press, 1987). I am also influenced in my overview by the book written by Michael Albert, et al., *Liberating Theory* (Boston: South End Press, 1986).

More recently, Prof. David Ray Griffin has been editing a series entitled "Constructive Postmodern Thought" which is demonstrating that there are certainly more options in the postmodern era than deconstruction or a return to some sort of fundamentalism; cf. David Ray Griffin, *God and Religion in the Postmodern World: Essays in Postmodern Theology* (Albany: SUNY Press, 1989). That aim I share. However, the books in Griffin's series are all deeply influenced by the process philosophy of Alfred North Whitehead and Charles Hartshorne. I was educated in Europe and my approach reflects the rational/existential perspective rather than a process perspective. I hope that this book here will be taken as a complement to the process approach.

2. Daniel Liechty, "Christian Freedom and Political Freedom," *Conrad Grebel Review*, Vol. IV (1986), pp. 101–23.

3. Cf. Hugh T. Kerr, "Trademarks of Theology," *Theology Today*, Vol. XLIII (1987), pp. 467–71.

1. A Starting Point for Religious Reflection

1. That religious reflection and thought must proceed from an awareness of crisis has been the theme of two different but related bodies of writing, those dealing with "post-Holocaust" theology, focusing on the history of antisemitism and genocide against the Jewish people of Europe, and "post-Hiroshima" theology, focusing on the human situation in the context of weapons of mass destruction. See for example the essays and literature in *Auschwitz: Beginning of a New Era? Reflections on the Holocaust*, ed. Eva Fleischner (New York: KTAV, 1977), and especially Steven T. Katz, *Post-Holocaust Dialogues: Critical Studies in Modern Jewish Thought* (New York: NYU Press, 1983), for the former, and Gordon D. Kaufman, *Theology for a Nuclear Age* (Philadelphia: The Westminster Press, 1985) for the latter. Other important works include Dale Auckerman, *Darkening Valley: A Biblical Perspective on Nuclear War* (Scottdale: Herald Press, 1989), and Christopher Grannis, Arthur Laffin and Elin Schade, *The Risk of the Cross: Christian Discipleship in the Nuclear Age* (New York: Seabury Press, 1981). Also, Andrew J. Weigert, "Christian Eschatological Identities in the Nuclear Context," JSSR vol. 27/2 (1988), pp. 175–91.

2. Cf. Eric Voegelin, *The New Science of Politics* (Chicago: University of Chicago Press, 1966).

3. In this I agree with the deconstructionist approach to theology, that in the first place the work of the theologian is iconoclastic. However, the theologian must eventually move beyond iconoclasm and, while retaining a strong sense of critical skepticism, begin to construct new understandings and formulations of responsible religious thought.

4. Ernest Becker, *The Denial of Death* (New York: The Free Press, 1973). For a penetrating extension of Becker's point of view, see Merold Westphal, *God, Guilt and Death* (Bloomington: Indiana University Press, 1987). For a more narrowly philosophical perspective on the same issue, cf. John Donnelly, ed., *Language, Metaphysics and Death* (New York: Fordham University Press, 1978), esp. pp. 25–31; 69–87; 106–15; 216–27.

5. Friedrich Nietzsche, *Beyond Good and Evil* (New York: Vintage Books, 1966).

6. Gabriel Vahanian, *No Other God* (New York: George Braziller, 1966).

7. This is one of the central and enduring phenomenological observations in Jean-Paul Sartre's *Being and Nothingness* (New York: Citadel, 1968).

8. Cf. here, for example, Sam Keen, *Faces of the Enemy* (New York: Harper & Row, 1986); Ernest Becker, *Escape from Evil* (New York: The Free Press, 1975); Richard Barnett, *The Giants* (Greenville: S & S Publishing, Inc., 1977); Ira Chernus, "The Symbolism of the Bomb," *Christian Century*, Oct. 12, 1983. Instructive here also is Troy Duster, "Conditions for Guilt-Free Massacre," in Nevitt Sanford and Craig Comstock, eds., *Sanctions for Evil: Sources of Social Destructiveness* (Boston: Beacon Press, 1971) pp. 25–36.

9. We do not have in America any developed "school" of the study of heretics. This is probably because, in the American context, it is very difficult to decide just what a heretic really is! However, in Europe, the study of "Ketzergeschichte" has a long history. While for centuries the evaluation of heretics was negative, there is also positive evaluation even among top scholars. Cf., for example, Walter Nigg, *Das Buch der Ketzer* (Zürich: Artemis Verlag, 1949) and the numerous essays collected in Hans Jürgen Schultz, ed., *Die Wahrheit der Ketzer* (Stuttgart: Kreuz Verlag, 1968).

2. The Ambiguity of Evil

1. Denis de Rougemont, "On the Devil and Politics," *Christianity and Crisis*, June 1941, reprinted in *Witness to a Generation*, Wayne H. Cowan, ed. (Indianapolis: Bobbs-Merrill Co., 1966), pp. 6–12.

2. Many names could be mentioned in this context: Charles Reich, Otto Rank, Norman O. Brown, Robert J. Lifton. I have relied most specifically on Paul Ricoeur, *The Symbolism of Evil* (Boston: Beacon Press, 1969); Ernest Becker, *The Structure of Evil* (New York: George Braziller, 1968) and *Escape From Evil* (New York: Free Press, 1975); Merold Westphal, *God, Guilt and Death* (Bloomington: Indiana University Press, 1984).

3. Becker, *Escape From Evil* (n.2), p. 96.

4. Paul Carus, *The History of the Devil and the Idea of Evil From the Earliest Times to the Present Day* (New York: Bell Publ. Co., 1969), is very informative.

5. This parallels closely the use of this concept, presented in a literary context, in René Girard, *Violence and the Sacred* (Baltimore: Johns Hopkins University Press, 1977), and *The Scapegoat* (Johns Hopkins University Press, 1986). Also from a theological point of view, see Raymund Schwager, SJ, *Must There Be Scapegoats? Violence and Redemption in the Bible* (San Francisco: Harper & Row, 1987).

6. That there is no shortage of religious leaders ready and willing to give God's blessing to the national conflict is confirmed in the study of Ray H. Abrams, *Preachers Present Arms* (Scottdale, Pa.: Herald Press, 1969).

7. Becker, *Escape from Evil* (n.2), pp. 150 and 153.

8. Sam Keen, *Faces of the Enemy: Reflections of the Hostile Imagination* (San Francisco: Harper & Row, 1986).

9. If I may be allowed one brief biographical digression: I left the United States for philosophical studies in Eastern Europe in 1978. At that time, Jimmy Carter was still a very popular President, especially among those of evangelical-leaning religious faith. I remained in Europe, migrating to theology, until late in 1986, just before the Iran/Contra affair was exposed to

the American people (although we knew of it in Europe as a rumor at least a year earlier). In short, I missed the entire "Reagan Era."

On my return to America, the thing that struck me most, and even now continues to boggle my mind, is the absolute and unbridled *greed* I see. And not only is this happening, but it is being held up to the American people as *good* and as something to be honored and emulated! A major company for years promised its workers that, if they did not unionize but rather trusted the company, they would be taken care of. Then a paper "takeover" occurred and whole branches of the company were sold off and closed down, with no thought whatsoever to the displacement of the workers who had been with the company into the third generation. The result was "profits" on the part of the banking consultants who organized the takeover, six- and seven-figure salaries, benefits and parachutes for the executives affected, and unemployment for the workers.

This was not the America I left, and it hurts deeply to see that we have gone this route. I can only hope that this "Reagan Era" was a short-term fluke. It is frankly frightening to teach in school the fall of the Roman Empire and at the same time read the daily papers! How demeaning that one of our country's most forthright economists, Lester Thurow, is reduced to cajolery of America's elite into acting (not with compassion and sacrifice for the sake of justice) *as* an elite, an elite which sees its own long-term interests served by education and investment, rather than as an "oligarchy" who continue to strive for the golden throne of a sinking ship! (Cf. Charles C. Mann, "The Man With All the Answers," *The Atlantic*, Vol. 265 No. 1, January 1990, pp. 45–62.)

The moral bankrupcy of the powers for evil in this "McTrump" phase of American history is obvious to the world. Let it become as obvious to us.

3. God in the Nexus of Human History

1. That the concept of God arises in the context of our search for meaning and purpose in life is backed from many different perspectives. I have been most influenced in this by Viktor Frankl and the "third Vienna school" of logotherapy. Cf. among the many works of Frankl especially his *Der unbewusste Gott: Psychotherapie und Religion* (Munich: Kösel-Verlag, 1977). Also, Reuven P. Bulka, *The Quest for Ultimate Meaning: Principles and Applications of Logotherapy* (New York: Philosophical Library, 1979). From a different perspective, but supporting the same point, cf. William Ernest Hocking, *The Meaning of Immortality in Human Experience* (New York: Harper & Brothers, 1957), and more recently James W. Fowler, *Stages of Faith: The Psychology of Human Development and the Quest for Meaning* (San Francisco: Harper & Row, 1981).

2. The ways in which people in America are coping with this need for a new frame of reference is the focus of the fascinating book by Robert N. Bellah, et al., *Habits of the Heart: Individualism and Commitment in American Life* (New York: Harper & Row, 1985). See also the companion volume of readings, *Individualism and Commitment in American Life* (New York: Harper & Row, 1987).

3. Claude S. Fischer and Christopher Lasch, "The Good Old Days," *TIKKUN*, Nov./Dec. 1988, pp. 69ff. Also Christopher Lasch, "Progress: The Last Superstition," *TIKKUN*, May/June 1989, pp. 27ff.

4. Antonio Gramsci, *The Modern Prince and Other Writings* (New York: International Publishers, 1957).

5. Among modern theologians, it is Gordon D. Kaufman who has pursued most consistently the theme of theology as a constructive task. See especially his recent books, *An Essay on Theological Method* (Missoula: Scholars Press, 1975), and *The Theological Imagination: Constructing the Concept of God* (Philadelphia: The Westminster Press, 1981). That theology is a matter of construction rather than description is also implied by many recent books by other authors. Very important here are Sallie McFague, *Models of God: Theology for an Ecological, Nuclear Age* (Philadelphia: Fortress Press, and London: SCM Press, 1987), and Charles S. McCoy, *When Gods Change: Hope For Theology* (Nashville: Abingdon Press, 1980). For the European perspective, the books of Jacques Pohier, *Quand je dis Dieu* (Paris: Editions du Seuil, 1977) and *God – in Fragments* (London: SCM Press, and New York: Crossroad Publishing Co., 1985), can be read to support this point of view, as well as the two volumes edited by Hans Küng and David Tracy, in which an international conference of ecumenical theologians came together to discuss the "paradigm shift" taking place on the theological scene. Cf. Küng/Tracy, eds., *Theologie-Wohin? Auf dem Weg zu einem neuen Paradigma* (Zürich and Gütersloh: Benziger Verlag and Gütersloher Verlagshaus Gerd Mohn, 1984) and *Das neue Paradigma von Theologie: Strukturen und Dimensionen* (Zürich and Gütersloh: Benziger Verlag and Gütersloher Verlagshaus Gerd Mohn, 1986). Of course the idea of "reality construction" was always implicit in the sociology of knowledge. Cf., for example, Burkart Holzner, *Reality Construction in Society* (Cambridge, MA.: Schenkman Publishing Company, 1967). It was only a matter of applying the insights of reality construction to theology for it to become explicit that theology is a constructive rather than descriptive effort. Perhaps it is most fitting then that Peter L. Berger, who with Thomas Luckman introduced many of us to the concept of reality as socially constructed, made just this application in his *The Heretical Imperative: Contemporary Possibilities of Religious Affirmation* (New York: Anchor/Doubleday, and London: Collins 1979).

4. The Example of Jesus

1. This theme comes through in no place so clearly as in the "Magnificat" of Mary, Luke 1:46ff. A systematic treatment has been given in J. P. M. Walsh, SJ, *The Mighty from Their Thrones: Power in the Biblical Tradition* (Philadelphia: Fortress Press, 1987). See also the essays collected in *God of the Lowly: Socio-Historical Interpretations of the Bible*, eds. Willy Schrottroff and Wolfgang Stegemann (Maryknoll: Orbis Books, 1984).

2. Cf. Norman K. Gottwald, *The Tribes of Yahweh: A Sociology of the Religion of Liberated Israel 1250–1050 BCE* (Maryknoll: Orbis Books, and London: SCM Press, 1979).

3. Norman K. Gottwald, "From Biblical Economies to Modern Economies,"

in *Churches in Struggle: Liberation Theologies and Social Change in North America*, ed. William K. Tabb (New York: Monthly Review Press, 1986), pp. 138–48.

4. Norman K. Gottwald, "Sociological Method in the Study of Ancient Israel," in *The Bible and Liberation: Political and Social Hermeneutics*, ed. N. K. Gottwald (Maryknoll: Orbis Books, 1983), pp. 26–37.

5. Cf. Frank Crusemann, *Der Widerstand gegen das Königtum: Die antiköniglichen Texte des Alten Testaments und der Kampf um den frühen israelitischen Staat* (Neukirchen: Neukirchen Verlag, 1978). Somewhat less to the point, but much better known, is Michael Walzer, *Exodus and Revolution* (New York: Basic Books, 1985).

6. Monotheism, of course, can also function as a religious support system for absolute monarchy – one God, one king. But so long as the loyalty to the ruler is ordered through loyalty to God, monotheism will finally stand as a relativizing factor to would-be tyrants. For a feminist perspective on this issue, cf. Marcia Falk, "Toward a Feminist Jewish Reconstruction of Monotheism," *TIKKUN*, July/August 1989, pp. 53ff.

7. Martin Hengel, *Property and Riches in the Early Church: Aspects of a Social History of Early Christianity* (London: SCM Press, and Philadelphia: Fortress Press, 1974).

8. This sense of living on through one's children is given very positive treatment by Robert Jay Lifton, *The Broken Connection: On Death and the Continuity of Life* (New York: Simon and Schuster, 1979), and also in his more recently published essays. An insightful comparison of Ernest Becker and Lifton on this point is Lucy Bregman, "Three Psycho-Mythologies of Death: Becker, Hillman and Lifton," *JAAR* LII/3 (1984), pp. 461–79.

9. See here especially John Howard Yoder, *The Politics of Jesus: Vicit Angus Noster* (Grand Rapids: Wm. B. Eerdmans, 1972); Martin Hengel, *Christ and Power* (Philadelphia: Fortress Press, 1977).

10. Cf. Yoder, *Politics* (n.9), pp. 26ff.; Martin Hengel, *Victory Over Violence: Jesus and the Revolutionaries* (Philadelphia: Fortress Press, 1973).

11. The importance of this tradition is most thoroughly discussed in Millard Lind, *Yahweh Is a Warrior: The Theology of Warfare in Ancient Israel* (Scottdale: Herald Press, 1980), pp. 91ff.

5. Toward a Critical Christology

1. Willi Marxsen, *Die Sache Jesu geht weiter* (Gütersloh: Gütersloher Verlagshaus Gerd Mohn, nd).

2. Cf. Thomas Sheehan, *The First Coming: How the Kingdom of God Became Christianity* (New York: Random House, 1986), pp. 175ff.; Edward Schillebeeckx, *Jesus: An Experiment in Christology* (London: Collins, and New York: Seabury Press, 1979), pp. 320ff.; Günther Bornkamm, "The Risen Lord and the Earthly Jesus: Mt. 28:16–20," in *The Future of Our Religious Past*, ed. James M. Robinson (New York: Harper and Row, and London: SCM Press, 1971), pp. 203–9.

3. Norman Perrin, *The Kingdom of God in the Teaching of Jesus* (London: SCM Press, and Philadelphia: The Westminster Press, 1963) and *Rediscovering*

the Teaching of Jesus (London: SCM Press, and New York: Harper and Row, 1967). Schillebeeckx, *Jesus* (n.2), pp. 105ff. Also very interesting in this regard are books being written by Jewish New Testament scholars, since these scholars are less likely than their Christian counterparts to interpret the texts recording the preaching of Jesus in traditionally Christian ways. See as one example Pinchas Lapide, *Er predigte in ihren Synagogen: Judische Evangelienauslegung* (Gütersloh: Gütersloher Verlagshaus Gerd Mohn, 1980).

4. Norman Perrin, "The Son of Man in the Synoptic Tradition,"*Biblical Research* XIII (1968), pp. 1–23; cf. also the essays in *The Historical Jesus and the Kerygmatic Christ*, eds. Carl Braaten and Roy Harrisville (Nashville: Abingdon Press, 1964); Sheehan, *First Coming* (n.2), pp. 183ff.

5. This view has been present in New Testament scholarship since the late nineteenth century. Recently it has been given theological treatment in Tom F. Driver, *Christ in a Changing World: Toward an Ethical Christology* (New York: Crossroad Publishing Company, and London: SCM Press, 1981). Cf. also Juan Luis Segundo, *An Evolutionary Approach to Jesus of Nazareth*, vol. V of *Jesus of Nazareth Yesterday and Today* (Maryknoll: Orbis Books, 1988).

6. Compare this view to Wilhelm Bousset, *Kyrios Christi* (Nashville: Abingdon Press, 1970). Although neither uses the terminology of a tactic of survival, and they discuss the issue specifically in relation to early Christian refusal to serve in the military, the view that the exclamation "Kyrios Christos" functioned in this capacity is strongly present in Adolf Harnack, *MILITIA Christi: The Christian Religion and the Military in the First Three Centuries* (Philadelphia: Fortress Press, 1981), and Jean-Michel Hornus, *It Is Not Lawful for Me to Fight: Early Christian Attitudes Toward War, Violence and the State* (Scottdale: Herald Press, 1980). Cf. also Ronald H. Bainton, *Christian Attitudes Toward War and Peace* (Nashville: Abingdon Press, 1960), pp. 66ff., and more recently James F. Childress, "Moral Discourse About War in the Early Church," in *Peace, Politics and the People of God*, ed. Paul Peachey (Philadelphia: Fortress Press, 1986), pp. 117ff.

7. That we are responsible for what we teach about Christ (rather than simply passers-on of received tradition) was made most clear to me by Tom Driver's chapter "Method for an Ethical Christology," in Driver, *Christ* (n.5), pp. 12ff.

8. My first formulation of what follows was presented in the context of Christian dialogue with Marxist perspectives on salvation. Cf. Daniel Liechty, "Free Church Assumptions in a Christian Approach to Marxism," *Conrad Grebel Review*, Vol. III (1985), pp. 211ff.

9. It is in this context again that we touch base with the current theme of the "priority of the poor" which is central to the so-called theology of liberation. A good example here is Leonardo Boff's book, *When Theology Listens to the Poor* (San Francisco: Harper & Row, 1988). This by no means should imply that the task of the theologian is simply to articulate in academic language and present as "truth" whatever religious ideas are present among the least powerful segments of the society. That segment of society holds many nasty and brutish religious notions. Not surprisingly, there is a strong messianic urge present. Cf. for example, Vittorio Lanternari, *The Religions of the Oppressed: A Study of Modern Messianic Cults* (New York: American Library, 1965).

Numerous other works could be cited for this point. It should, rather, be taken as a call to the religious thinker to search out among the least powerful segments of society that "principled atheism" toward the notions of God common to the powerful segments of society and to allow this principled atheism to function in a critical capacity in theological construction.

10. Schillebeeckx, *Jesus* (n.2), pp. 379ff.; Driver, *Christ* (n.5), pp. 32ff.; Sheehan, *First Coming* (n.2), pp. 206ff.

11. Recently Schubert Ogden has been taken to task for his formulations of a theology of liberation. The central focus of the complaint against him is that he must, finally, make a clear separation between "redemption" and "emancipation." Redemption is viewed as metaphysical redemption from "sin and death," while emancipation is viewed as liberation from concrete, present situations of unfreedom, cf. Anselm Kyongsuk Min, "How Not to Do a Theology of Liberation: A Critique of Schubert Ogden," *Journal of the American Academy of Religion* LVII/1, Spring 1989, pp. 83–102. The view I am presenting here, that we construct our teachings of being redeemed on an ethical stance toward the world, is, I think, immune to this criticism. Nevertheless, I think that Ogden is correct in insisting that some sort of "metaphysical" perspective on the human situation is a needed corrective in the struggle for emancipation. For myself, Jesus' relationship with the Zealot movement in his time is instructive. But like most of Jesus' teaching and example, it is not unambiguously conclusive. We must apply it in concrete situations. And that will entail agreements and disagreements.

12. The consummate statement of this view remains Oscar Cullmann, *Christ and Time* (Philadelphia: The Westminster Press, and London: SCM Press, 1950).

13. A criticism of sacramental theology from this perspective is offered in John Howard Yoder, *The Priestly Kingdom: Social Ethics as Gospel* (Notre Dame: University of Notre Dame Press, 1984).

14. The classic work is the monumental six-volume commentary by P. Billerbeck (and H. L. Strack), *Kommentar zum Neuen Testament aus Talmud und Midrasch* (Munich: C. H. Beck, 1922–1963).

15. According to a poster hanging in the hallway of the Vienna Meeting of the Religious Society of Friends, the following is attributed to George Fox: "Christ said this, the Apostles said that – but what canst thou say?" This captures exactly the message I am trying to express here.

16. The penetrating question posed by Tom Driver, *Christ* (n.5). Also helpful has been Paul F. Knitter, *No Other Name? A Critical Survey of Christian Attitudes Toward the World Religions* (Maryknoll: Orbis Books, and London: SCM Press, 1985).

6. Church Without Dogma

1. Therefore, for example, in relating to the English reader the richness of the world of the French peasant, author John Berger felt the need to include a lengthy foreword and afterword, drawing the reader into the thought-structure of the peasants (cf. his *Pig Earth*, New York: Pantheon Books, 1979). This is not because the English reader would not understand the *words*

of the stories – all were related in English. But Berger realized that without at least some limited attempt to bring to the English reader some window of understanding into the cultural context of the French peasants, an understanding of the stories themselves was impossible.

2. I assume words to be a subcategory of symbols. On the human being as a symbolic animal, see Ernest Becker, *The Birth and Death of Meaning: An Interdisciplinary Perspective on the Problem of Man* (New York: The Free Press, 1971), pp. 13ff. Some philosophers, such as Susanne Langer, have claimed that there are nondiscursive languages which have a kind of grammar structure but no semantic structure. Therefore, for example, people sharing no common language can communicate through music. This is probably true, but also assumes some common grounding in cultural experience. That music is meant to "communicate" at all is something that must be learned.

3. Anatol Rapoport, *Operational Philosophy: Integrating Knowledge and Action* (New York: Harper Brothers, 1954).

4. Ibid., pp. 193ff.

5. By spiritual life I mean inner experience of the world on which one can reflect, but which is never possible fully to articulate in language. Such attempts are always and only approximations (cf. Romans 8:26).

6. I have heard some objections as to why I place pacifism in such a central location in terms of ethics. It must be understood that I am speaking of pacifism in its broadest sense – that of a pacific (peaceful) approach toward life and others that does not assume that violent conflict is inevitable (and therefore does not prepare in advance for such conflict). It is an approach to life that always seeks reconciliation when conflict does occur, not punishment or revenge. It is much more than an abjuring of participation in armed conflict. Furthermore, genuine pacifists will disagree on specific ethical applications, such as medical, economic and social issues. Commitment to a pacifist ethic is no grounds for moral self-righteousness – as if all who disagree are immoral. It is unfortunate that because pacifists often express themselves in moralistic tones, they are perceived this way. A very good book applying this broader pacifist perspective to conflicts between nations is Duane K. Friesen, *Christian Peacemaking and International Conflict: A Realist Pacifist Perspective* (Scottdale: Herald Press, 1986). Friesen's work demonstrates clearly that a broader pacifist perspective, one which eschews moralisms and withdrawal, can be a very useful contribution. This needs to be expanded into other areas of ethics.

As to why I associate a pacifist stand toward the world with a genuine Christian ethic, I have no transcendental base of authority to "prove" it so. The tradition I grew up in strongly emphasized the theme of *Nachfolge Christi* (following the way of Jesus) as what it means to be a Christian. Perhaps this is somewhat simplistic, but it is difficult for me to conceive of the Christian life in any other terms. Following the way of Jesus, looking to Jesus as a model, integrating the "Jesus factor" into one's life – if there is no interest in that, even if it be only in terms of an integration dialectically conceived with some other norm, I cannot see the point in calling oneself Christian at all. And as I look at the portrait of the life of Jesus as it has been handed down to us by tradition, it seems inevitable to me that as one brings the "Jesus factor" into one's life, one will be moving toward an increasingly pacifist stand toward the world. At least I've yet to hear any argument that would convince me otherwise.

7. Cf. *A History of Christian Doctrine*, ed. Hubert Cunliffe-Jones (Edinburgh: T. & T. Clark, and Philadelphia: Fortress Press, 1980) pp. 21–190, and Arthur C. McGiffert, *A History of Christian Thought: Early and Eastern* (New York: Charles Scribners, 1932), contain good summaries of the early Christian controversies. In addition, many collections and investigations exist on individual points of controversy in the early church. Our knowledge of early Christian pluralism has been greatly extended by recent studies of extra-biblical writings. However, it is present within the biblical materials themselves.

8. Peter Munz, *Relationship and Solitude: A Study of the Relationship Between Ethics, Metaphysics and Mythology* (London: Eyre & Spottiswoode, 1964). In Munz's analysis, the symbol picture, or mythology, is a direct expression of spiritual experience. Metaphysics results from general observations about the symbol pictures taken compositely, i.e., metaphysical statements are *a posteriori*, synthetic statements and can be tested against the evidence of the symbol pictures. Also helpful on this point is Munz's more recent work, *The Shapes of Time: A New Look at the Philosophy of History* (Middletown: Wesleyan University Press, 1977).

9. On universalism, cf. Otto Weber, *Foundations of Dogmatics* (Grand Rapids: Wm. B. Eerdmans, 1983), Vol. II, pp. 451ff.; Hendrikus Berkhof, *Christian Faith* (Grand Rapids: Wm. B. Eerdmans, 1979), pp. 531ff.

10. Elaine Pagels, *The Gnostic Gospels* (New York: Random House, 1979). Also her more recent *Adam, Eve, and the Serpent* (New York: Random House, 1988).

7. In View of Other Religions

1. By conservatives I have in mind mainly the Protestant fundamentalists and neofundamentalists or evangelicals, simply because I know them the best. However, the same attitude of exclusivity would be found among Catholic traditionalists as well.

2. Cf. Gerald A. Anderson and Thomas F. Stransky, eds., *Mission Trends Number Two: Evangelization* (New York: Paulist Press, 1975), pp. 239–48, for the full text of the concluding document of this important 1974 meeting in Lausanne, Switzerland. This meeting has set the tone for evangelical missions, especially "youth" missions, since that time.

3. Barth's most clear statements are found in his *Church Dogmatics*, Vol. 1/2 (Edinburgh: T. and T. Clark, 1956) pp. 280–361. A shortened version is found in John Hick and Brian Hebblethwaite, eds., *Christianity and Other Religions* (Philadelphia: Fortress Press, 1980) pp. 32–51.

4. Rahner's *Theological Investigations* (London: Darton, Longman and Todd, and New York: Seabury Press) contain a few places where he speaks of this concept. Cf. for example, vol. 12, pp. 161–78; vol. 14, pp. 280–94.

5. Hans Küng, *On Being a Christian* (New York: Doubleday, and London: Collins, 1976) pp. 89–118; also *Theology for the Third Millennium: An Ecumenical View* (New York: Doubleday, 1988), pp. 227ff.

6. I am following here especially Hick's book *God Has Many Names* (Philadelphia: Westminster Press, 1982).

7. Ibid., pp. 45, 71, 114.

8. Ibid., p. 89.

9. Ibid.

10. Ibid., p. 92.

11. Ibid.

12. I do not wish to get bogged down in a defense of such theories and am happy to see these developmental stages not as hard scientific categories but rather as metaphors. I would acknowledge, however, the formative influence on my thinking of James W. Fowler's book *Stages of Faith: The Psychology of Human Development and the Quest for Meaning* (San Francisco: Harper & Row, 1981), and mostly through secondary sources the ideas of Lawrence Kohlberg.

13. People who involve themselves in interreligious ideas are much too quick to want to draw disparate sources into some kind of "higher synthesis." I do not take this to be the goal of interreligious dialogue at all. I tend to see it, in fact, as a result of our inability really to handle pluralism over the long run. We keep assuming there must be a higher synthesis somewhere and we are driven to find it. I would rather place any kind of synthesis on the back burner for a couple of generations. By then the natural mingling of traditions will perhaps make our concentrated efforts at finding a synthesis unnecessary. More open dialogue is goal enough for now, a dialogue that does not seek synthesis but rather peaceful coexistence. My views are strongly affected by the idea of "unitive pluralism" found in Paul F. Knitter, *No Other Name? A Critical Survey of Christian Attitudes Toward the World Religions* (Maryknoll: Orbis Books, and London: SCM Press, 1985).

8. Instead of a Conclusion

1. A needed perspective is offered by the articles "Four Studies of Church Growth and Decline" in the special March 1989 issue of JSSR. I hold this opinion on the overall decline of conservativism in America in spite of the fact that there has been a definite rise in conservative religious political voices on social issues in the recent past. This parallels the rise of a neoconservative politics in general, and not only in the United States. However I expect that the future of this new religious politics, like the Moral Majority itself, will be short-lived. The common ground which might be shared on a particular social issue will always be secondary to the groups' ideologies. The coalitions which fundamentalist-leaning people are able to form appear to me to be too fragile to endure. My views are also greatly influenced by David Martin, *A General Theory of Secularization* (New York: Harper & Row, 1978).

2. Ernst Bloch, *Naturrecht und menschliche Würde* (Frankfurt a.M.: Suhrkamp, 1977), p. 311.

3. Michael Harrington, *The Politics at God's Funeral: The Spiritual Crisis of Western Civilization* (Harmondsworth: Penguin Books, 1985).

4. Miguel de Unamuno, *The Tragic Sense of Life* (New York: Dover Publications, and London: SCM Press, 1954).

5. Paul Tillich, *Systematic Theology*, Vol. II (Chicago: University of Chicago Press, and London: SCM Press, 1957) pp. 208ff. Robert P. Scharlemann characterized this as Tillich's "no to Nothing" in a very illuminating article, "The No to Nothing and the Nothing to Know: Barth and Tillich and the Possibility of Theological Science," JAAR LV/1 (1987), pp. 57–74.

6. This has been the vision of many communal experiments, and, we might add, the very thing on which all but a small handful floundered. Finnegan's Rainbow is not easily achieved. A fascinating book from an insider's perspective is John Humphrey Noyes, *Strange Cults & Utopias of 19th century America* (New York: Dover Publishing, 1966, reprint of the 1870 edition of *History of American Socialism*).

7. Unamuno, Tragic Sense (n.4), pp. 297ff.

8. Cf. for example, the view presented in Johan Huizinga, *Homo Ludens: A Study of the Play Element in Culture* (Boston: Beacon Press, 1950). See also the various attempts to construct a "theology of play." Also very much to the point is the marvelous little book by James P. Carse, *Finite and Infinite Games: A Vision of Life as Play and Possibility* (New York: The Free Press, 1986).

INDEX